A GUIDE TO CHRISTIAN EUROPE

AUSTRIA

BELGIUM

FRANCE

GERMANY

GREAT BRITAIN

HOLLAND

IRELAND

ITALY

PORTUGAL

SPAIN

SWITZERLAND

A Traveler's Handbook of Castles
Cathedrals and Shrines
Heroes, Saints and Scholars
Europe Past and Present

A GUIDE TO CHRISTIAN EUROPE

C. J. McNASPY, s.j.

LOYOLA UNIVERSITY PRESS
Chicago   60657

ISBN 0-8294-0204-7

Matri

THE PREPARATION

THE PILGRIMAGE

THE
PREPARATION

INTRODUCTION

This little book is not meant for the professional traveler, who presumably has seen everything mentioned in it and much besides. Still less is it intended for the European, since the point of view here expressed is quite American. Besides, how can a native of any given country possibly be satisfied with a few pages, even if they are of unmitigated praise?

Nor does the book pretend to be literary in any recognizable sense. It cannot in any way enter into competition with the sort of thing Henry James and Hilaire Belloc did incomparably well in their time, or with what Sean O'Faolain, Aubrey Menen or Mary McCarthy do for us today.

Quite simply, it is meant to be a useful book. Not a narrowly utilitarian one: it doesn't tell you all about hotels, restaurants, currencies, medicines. Works of this kind are indispensable and indeed plentiful. Some of them are even excellent. I shall include several of these in the bibliography, quite aware that newer and superior ones may be coming out at any moment.

So much for what the book is not.

What it is, I find harder to say. But what it was designed to be was a sort of chatty, personal, informal set of hints or reminders for the person planning a first visit to Europe. If the tone at times is didactic and I seem to be "talking down," please overlook my ways or set them down to too many years of teaching and lecturing. With all the best intentions in the world, one can hardly escape his background.

However, some of the pedagogical (I hope not pedantic) manner is deliberate. For I am assuming that the normal reader doesn't keep his Survey of European History course right on tap, as if to face tomorrow's quiz. The slight glossary appended to the last chapter may seem intolerably obvious to some readers (for whom it is not intended), but useful, I hope, to many more. Again, a preoccupation with practicality.

Americans may go to Europe for any number of reasons and concatenations of reasons or pretexts. Happily, a European trip has become so common among college people as to be no longer a symbol of wealth or status, and, thankfully, the ugly tourist is fast becoming an anachronism. Serious, studious Americans, young people who have had to save and stint, now earnestly make what used to be called "The Grand Tour."

This "new tourism" tends to reduce snobbery and phoniness, but it does release the possibility of another error: a kind of cultural gluttony. Trying ravenously to devour every delight, one risks enjoying nothing. The pedantic Baedeker-bouncing from monument to monument, or canvas to canvas, that used to be caricatured as Teutonic, bids fair to becoming an American aberration.

Thus, in being selective—often at the cost of

omitting spots I really treasure—I have felt I was following the wiser and more helpful course. Plainly, if you have time to visit everything significant in a given country (say, if you have a whole year to spend on Holland alone), you will do better with *Baedeker* or the *Guide Bleu* series. My effort here has rather been to help you make an economical and feasible choice, assuming that your time is limited.

I have not lived long in Europe—not more than a couple of years. But I have visited there many times, inevitably preserving an American (though not, I trust, an America-First) outlook. For more than a decade I taught a general course in European history and another in the history of European art. Thus, principles of selectivity have here been based both on what I have personally witnessed and what I have studied. Though, inescapably, some countries and cities are more familiar and more sympathetic to me than others (and, doubtless, this will be evident throughout), I have treated, with few small exceptions, only those known to me at first hand. Thus, with considerable reluctance, I have not touched on Scandinavia, since I know it only from books and Ingmar Bergman. Otherwise, the book does deal with all the major countries of Western Europe.

The approach tends to stress the historical rather than the contemporary. This is not to suggest that Western Europe, as not a few isolationists liked to say until recently, is passé, finished. Quite the contrary. One of the most pointed lessons we can learn from Western Europe has to do with the present: how to live today without tearing up our roots.

The difficulty about thanking people is that if I were to name all those who have helped, this introduction would become more pretentious than it is, and would grow into a litany of friends. My confreres on the staff of *America* have shown more than brotherly forbearance; they have prodded, corrected, supported an undertaking that must have been harder on them than they showed. Nor can I ever sufficiently thank my revered tutor, Christopher Dawson, for initiating me, by the spoken and written word, into a love for the making and meaning of Europe. Another teacher and friend who showed me something of the Christian roots of Europe, sharing some of his own warm appreciation of Church history, is Father Gerald Ellard, S.J. I owe him more than I dare try to say here.

CJM

PLANNING

A pilgrimage need not be penitential, nor painful—nor even profitable, for that matter. But unavoidably it will be strenuous, and if it is to be strenuous it may as well be profitable. Other travel books (mentioned in the bibliography) will help relieve some of the strain and strenuousness. My purpose is to offer some suggestions that may help you decide ahead of time where to go, and how to make your investment in energy and money more rewarding from a spiritual point of view.

By "spiritual," here, I mean both the natural and the supernatural, the religious and the broadly cultural, the historical as much as the explicitly holy. For to visit Europe and not sense the deeply religious background is to see only the surface, and not all of the surface. While Europe has produced its spectacular villains, a more Christian—indeed, a more nearly true—approach is to recognize it as the continent of heroes and saints and their treasured shrines. I hope this does not seem naïve.

This wider and deeper viewpoint will not make your trip less enjoyable. Rather, I believe, the contrary. For, just as we usually get as much out of a visit as we bring with us, I believe that a very large part of the value of a trip lies in what we take home with us. "Rome puts demands on its visitors," observed journalist John Cogley. His statement applies to the rest of Europe as well.

Merely to have a fine time in the superficial sense, you need not bother to go to Europe at all. Surely there must be cheaper and more obvious places, as well as more sophisticated ones, where you can be confident of the right kind of food and accommodation, as well as a completely familiar language. However, if you expect to make your trip the joy of a lifetime, something you will treasure for years to come, you will have to make discriminate choices.

Choices evidently imply rejections, since every time we select certain values we forgo others. Two enticements that face the prospective pilgrim are: (1) to try frenziedly to see everything, and (2) to become beguiled by the sirens of European *joie de vivre*. In answer to the first, be reminded that you must choose, even more austerely than the book has already chosen. In answer to the second, try to remember all the further and deeper and more lasting joys that you can carry home.

Ever so much will depend, too, on how much time you can afford to dedicate. If it is only two weeks, of course, you can live at a very intense pace, without any rest days. But if it is to be two months, then you will have to allow time for relaxation and rebuilding.

"Oh, must we see *another* cathedral?" was the weary complaint I overheard an anguished husband address to his culture-bound wife. The greatest of cathedrals, even Chartres itself, can prove a crashing bore to the sated soul. Some freshness is forever needed. Be warned by Mark Twain (allowing for his skill in hyperbole): "I do not want Michelangelo for breakfast—for luncheon—for dinner—for tea—for supper—for between meals. I like a change, occasionally."

Again different temperaments and ages can endure different tempi. When choosing your travel companions, make some allowance for this. Or, at least, if you can't find companions who move at approximately your pace, make sure that you are both understanding enough to be able to go your separate ways, at least on occasion. I am assuming, of course, some community of interest and viewpoint, since its absence would doom the trip from the start. This implies, too, some latitude for individual tastes and caprice, since one man's zest is another's ennui. To pretend the contrary will lead nowhere.

Age, health, talent and disposition will converge to dictate certain arrangements: whether, for instance, you travel in an organized group, or with one or two friends, or alone. Few young men, it need hardly be said, would enjoy the prospect of being a solitary man in a troupe of however amiable spinsters. The non-gregarious and some of the very gregarious may also enjoy going alone: the non-gregarious relishing solitude, and the very gregarious being gifted at making friends quickly anywhere, especially if they possess some knack at languages. Four congenial people can economically buy a car in Europe and sell it after the trip; however, traveling by car presupposes plenty of time and the ability to endure the close presence of the same people over long stretches.

While this book is geared especially to a long-ish trip, at least one of several months, I shall venture to propose an outrageous but possible two-week program—one that, surprisingly, has proved satisfactory to several friends who were willing to try it. It obviously presupposes that you will do almost all travel by plane.

Following this preposterous plan involves flying first to London, spending two days there and one at Oxford, which you will reach by train. Then allow three days in Paris, including one for Char-tres, going and returning to Chartres by train. Then fly to Lourdes and spend the day there (in sum-mer there are flights almost every day, but check this before you leave). Then fly to Madrid, where you visit the Prado that afternoon; the next day take the Avila-Escorial-Valley of the Fallen bus tour; the next day the Toledo tour. The next day fly to Rome, spend as many days there as possible and finally return to America.

Fatuous, of course. And what of Venice, Flor-ence, Vienna, Seville, Bruges and Assisi? Not on a two-week trip. But you will have seen and thrilled to half a dozen of Europe's greatest shrines, at least eight of its most splendid ca-thedrals, and some four of the five or six most precious museums in the world. Can even the most omnivorous and sturdy nervous system ab-sorb more than this in a fortnight?

But if you have more time and want to travel

most thriftily, Europe has an incredible arrangement for unlimited first-class railway travel. For one month you buy a pass usable in any Western country, for $110; for two months $150; for three months $180. Very economical.

Even if you take the blitz-tour described above (from which I have attempted to discourage you), you will do well to remember that any pilgrimage involves contemplation. You cannot "do" Lourdes in a non-contemplative mood: you need time to savor and pray and join the immense sacred and social experience of the processions. In the same way, St. Peter's and the Catacombs are less than worthless to the trivial, unprayerful eye. Such holy places are really seen only by the soul, and best contemplated from a kneeling position. They are much too meaningful to be rushed through like Times Square. The same is true of Avila, Westminster, the Holy Chapel, Chartres—all of which must be relished, not just glimpsed.

A few more gentle reminders may be in order here before you enter your European novitiate. One is that it would be naïve to think of Europe simply as old and ourselves as new. Actually, of course, no European country today is living under a form of government as ancient as ours. The British, for example, have modified their unwritten constitution so drastically during the past two centuries that it must be recognized as thoroughly different. Far less change has occurred to ours, even after our Civil War and the move toward centralization. France, Italy, Spain, Germany, Holland,

Belgium, Portugal, Ireland, and even stable Switzerland (now operating under its 1848 [recast in
1874] Constitution), have all changed governments
—some many times, some quite drastically—since
we adopted our Constitution back in 1789. Only
the Vatican can be said to be as politically ancient
as the United States; indeed, it is many times older.
Yet, think of how the Papal States have changed
in the past century—losing all territory in 1870
and regaining only a few acres in 1929.

In other matters too Europe has changed even
more than we have. I am referring not only to
the "Miracle of Europe," that enormous rebuilding after World War II. Take social reform, for
example. The old exploitation of workers that so
obsessed Marx while he was studying in England
has long since been remedied by social legislation,
which, in many European countries, antedated
ours and still goes considerably beyond it. In this
regard, many Western Europeans, even apart from
doctrinaire Socialists, think of Americans as old-
fashioned, if not archaic, in their social viewpoints.
This attitude may shock you the first time you
encounter it.

A bit more surprising, possibly, to some Americans is the European development in religious matters. Christianity did not come to an end in Europe
with the building of Gothic or baroque churches—
even granted, as Robert Louis Stevenson felt, that
"mankind was never so inspired as when it made
a cathedral."

The Church is not medieval, even if some of her customs and regalia remain so. With perennial vitality, she has continually renewed herself; and quite often it is precisely in ancient lands, as in France, her "eldest daughter," that she has made the most striking contemporary adaptations. Many of the vibrant movements that are just now being felt in America were initiated in France, Belgium, Germany or Holland. In the "dialogue" among Christians, for example, and in the liturgical renewal, these countries can offer us a good deal to think about and imitate. Often enough, behind traditional, staid façades, like those of Saint-Séverin or Chartres or Maria Laach, you will discover Christians vigorously in tune with our century. In fact, often you will find them more "in touch" than Christians closer to home.

Thus, if European devotion has not been stressed here, it is rather because a book that sets out to do everything does nothing. Very likely, I grant, too much has been attempted as it is. But my purpose throughout has been to refresh your sense of Western Europe before you start—to help you recall Europe's sacred and deeply human roots.

Now, take out a world map or globe. Draw your finger around the twelve small (only physically small) countries that you are to visit. Then realize, if you can, what an astonishing concentration of Christian and human accomplishment—what variety amid unity—what intense quality and un-

imaginable quantity—is packed into this tiny
corner of the earth, from which so much has
radiated almost everywhere. Then plan your
Christian-Humanist pilgrimage and expect it to be
the most inspiring episode of your life.

GOING HOME
TO EUROPE

If you must be miserly about time, flying to and from Europe instead of going by ship, you miss some precious, bittersweet moments. On the way over, you will find the approach too instantaneous and unprepared; it seems downright indecent to cross an entire ocean without a sense of distance. And on the way back, from the moment you enter Orly or Barajas or the London Airport, you suddenly find yourself in that faceless, colorless, tasteless world of the identical. Already you have abruptly left Europe. You could be anywhere, except in Europe, the continent of diversity. Then you are whisked aboard, with no time for a last look, much less time to think and tie the wondrous experience together. You doze off, only to wake, half-drugged, in another impersonal airport that again might be anywhere. Then, instantly, back into the humdrum, with no chance for reflection and assimilation. And no chance to start planning your next trip to Europe.

What does such a trip mean to the adult American today? Is it a temporary flight from reality— the type indulged in by some of our cultural forebears, who recoiled from the crassness and tough-

ness of American life? Or is it a bohemian escape
from philistinism and the grind of sameness? Or
isn't it, rather, a return to roots? Granted, the
roots are not the plant, and we are not exactly
Europeans. But we can hardly know what we are,
spiritually and humanly, without knowing something of what Europe is. Hence, we study European history as our own. Hence, too, our laboratory experience—our European pilgrimage.

We call Europe a "continent," largely because
it is hard to know what to call it. It is, of course,
not a continent in the sense that Africa or the two
Americas are continents. If ever the jest about
"So-and-so not being a place but a state of mind"
was true, Europe is, par excellence, that place. The
map shows it to be just a peninsula of the vast
land mass of Asia. But it is a special kind of peninsula—all gnarled and subdivided and full of sub-
peninsulas, highly articulated and rich in counte-
nance.

When we look more closely at the map we find
all kinds of man-made markings, political divisions and subdivisions, clusters of cities, all linked
(and separated) with lines that remind us of mag-
netic lines of force. And so they are. Few areas in
all the world are so threaded with human com-
munications, so richly and diversely populated;
and none, we may safely guess, is so "hominized."

As you fly, say, from Paris to Amsterdam, you
are never out of sight of some twenty villages.
Castile and La Mancha have their barren spots,
but even there you are always in reach of ancient

castles and windmills and modern dams. I am not one to belittle the majesty of mountains, but what struck me most about European mountains—Alps, Pyrenees, Apennines—was not their immensity as much as their beauty, their relatively civilized look, their closeness to man. Somehow, even they, in all their glory, seemed made to the measure of man, almost man-made.

Historians have not overlooked the comparative smallness of Europe its features or the variety within this smallness. One of them (Oscar Halecki) has asserted that "whatever is colossal and uniform is definitely un-European, and that is the secret of all the refinement and distinction of European civilization." He may be pushing the point a bit, for seldom does one factor account for so much. But there is more than coincidence, I believe, in the fact that so many small European countries are important and have made enormous "individual cultural contributions to a common patrimony."

When you discover for yourself that England is no bigger than Mississippi, Austria smaller than Indiana, and the whole of Italy not as large as New Mexico, you will remember values other than size. Visiting little Portugal, I recalled with some surprise that this tiny land once conquered a great part of the world and produced a literature of world renown. There is an *Oxford Book of Portuguese Verse,* but I have not yet seen an *Oxford Book of Dakotan Verse,* though either of the Dakotas is roughly twice the size of Portugal.

There is a considerable Catalan literature, though
Catalonia is now only a province of Spain. And
how many countries in the world have produced
painting to match that of the Netherlands (one
fifth the size of Oklahoma)? Granted we are com-
paring only size, not population or history or other
cultural traits; but the point, so far as it goes, is
illuminating.

But we must not slip into megalomania in re-
verse. If size is not the most significant value,
neither is smallness supreme. Else, why has not
Paraguay, one of South America's smallest countries, been culturally productive? Or Honduras, or
Estonia, or Greece in recent years, for that matter?
Or, even more importantly, Europe itself before a
certain moment in history? Those who want to
interpret all of history and culture in terms of geographical determinism are no better off (when it
comes to accounting for all the facts) than those
who have some neat racial theory. For it is a com-
monplace that the same areas and the same na-
tionalities have, during the course of world history, played major and minor roles—have been
successively in the vanguard and the rear of civilization.

What we think of as Europe (and here I am
concerned only with that part of Europe that we
easily visit, Western Europe, "uncurtained" Europe) is thus not as much a geographical entity as
a cultural one. It is, in Christopher Dawson's
words, "a man-made continent, an historical creation, an invention."

Since most of us Americans are not blood-descendants of the Greeks or Romans, still less of the Egyptians, Persians or Mesopotamians, we find it unflattering to be reminded that our ancestors were known as "barbarians" until a relatively short time ago. For a moment we may be comforted by the explanation that "barbarian" did not mean then what it has come to mean. However, in the most generous and coldly scientific sense, they were, by and large, considerably less than what is called fully civilized. Not having invented writing, they had only the most conservative, not creative, collective memories. Cities they did not know. (The word "city" and the word "civilized" have a common origin in a word that means "citizen.") Their culture was tribal, roughly at the level of the Iroquois in the eighteenth century, their villages being immeasurably less developed than Harappa, Mahenjo-Daro and other Indus Valley cities that go back some thousands of years before Christ.

How then did "the old country," our ancestral Europe, come to possess civilization? A number of celebrated historians have addressed themselves to the question, and their answers have much in common. The Swiss scholar, Gonzague de Reynold, has written as much as anyone on the meaning and make-up of Europe. He likes to think of the ancient Middle-Eastern civilizations (Egypt and the Fertile Crescent, in particular) as "Pre-Europe." While from the viewpoint of these ancient civilizations this approach seems narrow and chauvinistic, from the European and American position it makes sense. For very many of the values that we prize most did exist in these areas; and though precisely how much they really contributed to us is still obscure, no one doubts the fact of some contribution. And so, we still start our study of history with Egypt and Mesopotamia. Every child knows that somehow the Pyramids belong to him.

Much closer to us, and actually on what we call the continent of Europe, is M. de Reynold's "Proto-Europe," the world of Greece. This world, of course, was not restricted to the tiny area of the Balkan peninsula that we call Greece today. It included many islands, and quickly came to embrace a large part of southern Italy and Sicily, together with considerable beachheads all over the Mediterranean. Marseilles and Barcelona, we recall, were once Greek cities, and while little of Greek architecture stands there (and poignantly little even in Athens), even today we sense some mysterious continuity with that "Proto-European" world. It is the same Mediterranean sky and water, piercingly blue and luminous—in sight of which most Greeks, save possibly the austere Spartans, always lived.

It is no longer stylish to speak of the "Greek Miracle." But, miracle or no, the Greek experience has gone deep into the European (and our) soul. Paul Valéry may have been very French and absurdly provincial when he said, "There are the Greeks and ourselves." Yet it is only the exclusiveness of the phrase that shocks, and the fact that we, and not others, are included with the Greeks. Even so, I found it embarrassing to open a Sanskrit dictionary and learn that the ancient Hindus used the word *yavana* to mean Greek *and* barbarian—a salutary lesson against any kind of cultural parochialism.

Minimize their accomplishment as we may like, we can hardly doubt that the Greeks questioned and explored nearly every human problem. Quite naturally they came up with more questions than answers, but usually, at least, they asked the right questions and asked them in a rational and orderly way. If we find their answers simple and lacking in a number of dimensions, we do admire their Mediterranean love of clarity. If their art seems all too human in its attempt and its success, it does present attainable norms, a sense of measure and the very concept of limits that we know as classical.

Without rhapsodizing in the mood of Pericles in his much-quoted funeral oration, and always remembering the deep deficiencies of Greek social and political life, we can understand René Grousset's appraisal: "The Greek genius represents, in all domains and for the first time, the liberation of the human spirit." Thus, if Europe is a community of peoples enjoying a common cultural heritage, while preserving a large measure of individuality and regional diversity, then Greece may be thought of not only as a "Proto-Europe," but even as a "Micro-Europe."

The next element in the making of Europe was, of course, Rome. It is obviously regrettable to speak of a "next element," as though each of these elements was in some way equivalent or parallel to the others. Rome's contribution is partly like Greece's, and partly very unlike it. In content it may, indeed, be almost insignificant in comparison. For very much of what we think of as "classical" is ultimately of Greek, rather than Roman, issue. Even when we refer to Roman law and government as ours, we remember that, while the word "republic" is Roman, the terms "democracy," "monarchy," "aristocracy," and all the other "-ocracies" are Greek. Moreover, the final codification of Roman law took place under Justinian in the Greek capital of the Roman Empire, Constantinople.

We are Roman in more than our law and politics, for through Rome and from Rome we (that is, our European fathers) received Mediterranean civilization. Dawson begins the making of Europe with Caesar's conquest of Gaul, and his reasons are not hard to see.

If Greece symbolizes the diversity of Europe, Rome with its strong sense of unity amid variety gave the future Europeans (for up to then they were simply Celts, Franks and other kinds of "barbarians") a sense of Europe. Even the Germanic invaders came to look upon the decaying Empire not so much as something to be pillaged as something to be shared in. Their chieftains gloried in brandishing good Roman titles like prefect, praetor and consul. To them, the Empire became a career.

Caesar's conquest of Gaul, like most other Roman gains in Europe, was not a fly-by-night accomplishment. The Romans were builders (the lapidary phrase "Balbus built a wall" has been taken as symptomatic of the Roman approach). They were not mere adventurers (as Homer describes his hero, Odysseus), curious, inquiring, resourceful; they could hardly match the Greeks in fine arts or philosophy, as Virgil in a patriotic sentence grants; but "their arts were to rule over nations, to establish peace, to be generous to the conquered, to defeat the haughty."

Pre-eminently, they were empire builders, and it is more than coincidental that many Roman buildings—roads, walls, bridges, viaducts, sewers, aqueducts, arenas, baths and temples—still stand and serve their honest function. Anyone who goes to Europe may see performances in Roman theaters even today, and bullfights in Roman arenas. And those great, arrow-straight Roman roads are still in use. Once, driving in England before the new superhighways were built, I remarked how straight a particular stretch of road was. "Oh, this is the old Roman road," my British friend explained.

There's a bit of conversation in Evelyn Waugh's *Helena* that expresses as vividly as anything I know the meaning of Rome. Helena asks her husband, the future emperor Constantius, if there must always be a wall. Constantius replies that, although he is not a sentimental man, he loves the wall. "Think of it, mile upon mile, from snow to desert, a single great girdle round the civilized world; inside, peace, decency, the law, the altars of the gods, industry, the arts, order; outside, wild beasts and savages, forest and swamp, bloody mumbo-jumbo, men like wolf-packs; and along the wall the armed might of the Empire, sleepless, holding the line. Doesn't it make you see what The City means?" Helena wonders if Rome will ever go beyond the wall, into the wild lands. "Instead of the barbarian breaking in, might The City one day break out?" When Constantius scoffs that she's been reading Virgil, Helena responds: "Couldn't the wall be at the limits of the world and all men, civilized and barbarian, have a share in The City?"

The reverie actually did come true to a degree. But the dynamic element that brought it to pass was not simply the Roman ideal. It came from Christianity. During the era that we think of as the Dark Ages, "ancient civilization," as Gonzague de Reynold puts it, "was worn out; the Roman Empire dislocated; barbarians were masters of the West but unable to save the situation and to rebuild." Using the metaphor of a house, he refers to the ground floor when speaking of the Greek and pre-Greek part of our civilization, to the second floor as Rome, to the third as the era of barbarian invaders, and to Christianity as the roof. "The Church took spiritual charge not only of souls but of whole peoples," baptizing the barbarians not only into Christians but into sharers in the accumulated values of classical antiquity.

Dawson sums up his exploration into the making of Europe in this sentence: "The formation of Western Christendom by the conversion of the barbarians and the transmission to them of the tradition of Mediterranean culture by the Church marks a new stage in the Western development and the birth of the new European society of nations."

Europe's birth was prolonged and painful, and, as so often in human things, came about as a by-product of something else. The missioners and monks who civilized the barbarians were not principally interested in saving civilization; they were saving souls. It is hard for us today to form anything like a true picture of what the monasteries meant between the years, say, 500 and 1000. They were not merely citadels of holiness in an only half-converted world, oases of sanity and decency in what must have seemed a desert, bastions of learning much like the later universities; they were creative nuclei, from which sturdy monks went forth to convert, to domesticate, to humanize. Dawson (and many other historians) refer to monasticism as having had "a greater and more direct influence on the formation of Christian culture than any other single factor." He further points out the unique influence of the monastery "on the new Christian society of the barbaric North, where there was no tradition of city culture . . . where the coming of the monks meant not only a new religious way of life but a new civilization." J. Décarreaux, in his magisterial new work, *Les Moines et la Civilisation,* puts into penetrating focus the scope of our debt to St. Benedict and his spiritual sons.

The monastery was a center of culture in another way that we, with our secularized attitude toward culture, are prone to overlook. As the center and, in great part, the source of the liturgy, it wedded Christian life and worship with Roman dignity. What the cathedral would become during the Middle Ages (say, from 1000-1450), the monastery was in this earlier formative period: the place where God's people could gather in security, under God's aegis, to worship and receive the Word.

One might be inclined to wonder at the vastness of effort that went into Mont-Saint-Michel, Vézelay, Monte Cassino, if one forgot the complex role the monasteries played. Before the rise of the university, the monastery was explicitly *the* preserver and promoter of learning. In it, as well as in cathedral and church, statuary, mosaic, fresco, and stained glass were more than adornments to produce a sacral atmosphere; they were, to a great extent, directly pedagogical in a day of limited literacy.

After Constantine moved his capital to Byzantium (renamed, of course, Constantinople) in 330, and especially after 476, traditional date of the fall of Rome (when Romulus Augustulus was deposed by Odoacer), though the spiritual capital remained in Rome, the See of St. Peter, the political and cultural center of the West began to move. At one time it would be Milan, at another Ravenna, where even today an overwhelming proportion of the glories of Byzantine culture are preserved.

Again, in the nascent world of Europe, for some years several cities of Spain were leaders, until the capture of Spain by the Moslems (especially the decisive battle of Jérez de la Frontera, 711). Northward the Moslems moved, until in 732 they were thrown back by Charles Martel in one of the most important battles of Western history, fought somewhere near Poitiers and Tours (ironically— such are the vagaries of history—we don't know exactly where).

Charles Martel's grandson, known to history as Charlemagne, became a new Roman Emperor of the West and was so crowned by the Pope, at Rome on Christmas Day, 800. This date is a good, round and meaningful number to remember, for with the crowning of Charlemagne, the area now known as France and Western Germany became the most dynamic of Western Europe. Though Charlemagne had no capital as such, it is not fanciful to regard Aachen (where he is buried) as one of Europe's important, symbolic cities.

Charlemagne's new Roman Empire was premature and not destined to survive. The concept did survive, however; historians see in medieval Christendom the extension and fulfillment of the Carolingian dream. Between 1000 and 1300 West-

ern Europe became an important civilization, seeing the rise of the European city (in direct continuity with the great modern cities that we know
today), the European state (again, the same in
area as certain modern states, at least in broad
outlines), the estates of parliament, the universities, chivalry, the cathedrals, and much of the
finest Christian philosophy and poetry.

Meanwhile Spain was being regained for Christendom by the slow Reconquista which absorbed
her energies and instilled a number of character
traits in her peoples. Central and much of Eastern
Europe too were being brought into the society of
nations that we call Europe—nations like Poland,
Hungary, Lithuania. However, in 1054 was con-
summated the disastrous schism between East and
West, from which Christendom has never fully
recovered. At the end of the Middle Ages with the
Reformation came another tragic division, when,
roughly speaking, Northern Europe broke from
Rome.

Whether or not we should speak of the Renaissance as one or many movements, it seems characteristic of vital cultures from time to time to
generate unpredictable bursts of energy from
within. Charlemagne's day is known as the Carolingian Renaissance; the twelfth century is often
thought of as a Renaissance; and so is the thirteenth. These bursts are perhaps better thought of
as "quickenings," since, though there is an element
of "rebirth," each of them is more than a return
to the past. But when we speak of *the* Renaissance

we will, of course, think of Florence as its center; just as when we speak of the flowering of the Middle Ages, we naturally think of Paris as its capital.

The explosion of scientific and geographical exploration that characterized the fifteenth and sixteenth centuries left its lasting mark on Europe. New worlds were there to conquer, both in science laboratory and in the vaster laboratory of a widened earth. Though many a European went as missionary from the highest and purest motives, explorers were more often than not in search of gold and trade and regions to colonize. Science and many technological applications of science began to spiral upwards, and these helped to give Europe its position of prestige and power that was taken for granted until recent decades.

It took some time before Europe and America, its daughter, became indistinguishable as the Atlantic Community. The Baroque Age, with its superb vitality, was not long-lived, and from the Christian viewpoint suffered from too close dependence on certain monarchs. Nevertheless, it too produced precious fruits of sanctity and Christian culture. Happily past are the days when one looked down one's nose on anything baroque; but if anyone should be so tempted, he may hardly do better than make a close study of E. I. Watkin's *Catholic Art and Culture,* preferably before setting out for Europe.

Most of the later movements of European culture are shared with America—the Enlightenment,

the Revolutionary Era, the Industrial Revolution
and the whole experience of the nineteenth and
twentieth centuries. These movements are fascinating to study, but since they are as much American
as European, they can hardly be the main objects
of a pilgrimage to Europe.

A final note of caution. Europeans have known
suffering on a scale that Americans find hard even
to conceive. At times, then, they may strike us as
apparently disillusioned, skeptical, jaded, perhaps
weary of life. Although attitudes have bettered
considerably since World War II, they may still
shock the unwarned.

However, if we are willing to see the bright side
and to be impressed by Europe's recovery, we will
find ourselves again and again astonished. For
everywhere in Western Europe we observe an energy and creativity today that are hard to match,
even in Europe's long, exciting history. Granted
that some of this may be credited to American aid,
it would be ungracious (and inaccurate) of us to
overstate the case, and still more to mimimize
the initiative and industry that brought this aid to
full achievement. In contemporary architecture,
for example, we shall find fresh ideas that may
even make us feel that much recent American
building appears dully standardized. And, more
importantly, the Common Market—doubtless one
of the most colossal steps forward in all of history
—is one of our century's true glories.

Once again, after several tragic decades, Europe
has emerged as the continent of initiative, of imag-

ination, of non-conformity, of measure and proportion, of constructive individualism, of what Péguy called "liberated intelligences." If we still have much to give Europe—as I believe we do—Europe still has a great deal to offer us, provided we are modest and wise enough to accept.

THE PILGRIMAGE

SPAIN

The exciting touristic event of the past decade
has been the discovery of Spain, not only by
Americans but by Europeans too. Never has so
remarkable a country suffered from such a "bad
press" abroad. The "Black Legend"—Spain's
unreserved iniquity—has been refuted again and
again by serious historians, but somehow the
refutation has seldom managed to seep down to the
level of popular journals or textbooks.

However, what may ultimately do more to re-
store Spain's due reputation than all the scholarship in the world is the exchange value of the
peseta. For as long as it is kept down, prices will
remain down for visitors; and visitors will gladly
overcome their prejudices when money favors.
Even the French, traditionally contemptuous of
their neighbor beyond the Pyrenees, have begun
to rectify their ways, and we Hispanophiles have
found a good deal of satisfaction watching sophisticated French tourists literally gasping at the un-
suspected splendor of a Salamanca façade, a
Velázquez in the Prado, the utter splendor of
Toledo. Spain has now become a fairly close second to Italy as a tourist and pilgrim attraction.
Ruled in turn by Phoenicians, Carthaginians,
Romans, Moors and Catholics, it has inherited
an untold variety of cultural treasures.

MADRID

Madrid, where you will almost surely land if you come by plane, is an odd capital. It is, by European standards, an upstart among cities, almost as devoid of venerable historical associations as Washington. For, as a French tourist guide published in 1908 put it, "Madrid, like a star amid the other Spanish cities, has been refused by nature practically all the conditions necessary for the development of a great city." Instead, it is the creation of a headstrong king, Philip II, and a determined people. The Conquistadors not only quelled Aztec and Inca; they mastered the rugged bleakness of New Castile, creating a city where none should be.

Thus Madrid is a "city against nature," an "act of historic willpower," a "gigantic artifice," "sheer vitality," "built rather than born." So Laín Entralgo, one of Spain's greatest living thinkers, sees Madrid. It is a city every traveler comes to love.

However, it is a poor city for the *pilgrim*. Here almost everything is modern (not *modern* modern, but eighteenth- and nineteenth-century modern), with hardly a shrine worth mentioning. You will, of course, find Madrid a pleasant place to rest and recuperate between shrines. And if your tastes run at all toward painting, the **Prado** may very well become your best loved of all museums. As mammoth galleries go (the Louvre or New York's Metropolitan) it is small and selective, but of a sustained quality that makes its larger rivals seem overblown. For some 2972 works of art do not make an impressively large museum in terms of sheer numbers.

However, how many cities can point to nine of Raphael's finest paintings? And where else can one find the whole Spanish school? In the Prado you will see virtually all the major canvases of Velázquez, Ribera and Goya (except for the Goyas in the church San Antonio de la Florida, also in Madrid) as well as the finest of Zurbarán, Murillo and El Greco (apart from their works in nearby Toledo). As you contemplate "Las Meninas," for example, or "The Third of May," or "Las Hilanderas," or "The Descent of the Holy Spirit," or a hundred other masterworks, you wonder whether you have ever previously been initiated into Spanish painting.

For Madrid's Royal Palace, the gracious Retiro Park, the lordly Plaza Mayor and much else, you will need little help. They are as transparent as the Madrid sky. Meanwhile, you may also use Madrid as an ideal center from which to visit its more historic and impressive neighbors—the Escorial, Avila, Toledo, Segovia.

THE ESCORIAL

This colossal pile of granite makes other palaces seem frivolous or trivial. A monastery, a Versailles and a Pyramid of Cheops combined, it defies category or criticism. To say it is cold is not quite

fair. Austere, majestic, perhaps even forbidding—
but very moving. The architect who completed the
building, Juan de Herrera, had a sure feeling for
mass, scale, proportion (if you have seen the great
cathedral of Puebla, Mexico, you know his style
and are ready to cope with the Escorial). The
central dome rises to a height that challenges St.
Peter's, and everything about the building makes
it as imposing as any structure in the world. (My
notes remind me that the outer walls are nine to
ten feet thick, all solid granite.)

King Philip II (one of the most tragic and con-
troverted characters in history) had the Escorial
built as a residence and a monastery, where prayer
would ceaselessly go up to heaven for his empire.
It is still an active monastery, but Philip's own
rooms—from which you can always see the altar
—are not in use. The chapel is a repository of
relics from many saints, and within the sacristy
and library you will find impressive collections of
sacred painting by the Spanish masters.

Most awesome, however, is the Royal Pantheon
—the vast mausoleum, built under the altar, containing the bodies of most of the royalty of Spain
from Charles V (Philip's father) to Alfonso XIII.
In stately, identical marble sarcophagi lie the kings
and queens of Spain, all alike in death. In nearby
vaults, somewhat lighter in style, are the tombs of
princes and infantas, those who did not achieve
kingship; and perhaps most memorable of all is
the special grave of Don Juan (not the rascal of
opera and legend, but the illegitimate half-brother

of Philip, the hero of the Battle of Lepanto, famed in history and G. K. Chesterton's stirring poem. You will catch yourself whispering some of those ringing lines).

For a superb exterior view, you may drive up the nearby mountain, or better still, go to the spot traditionally called the "Seat of Philip the Second," where the monarch is said to have watched the progress of the building. There you may use the alleged seat of royalty.

THE VALLEY OF THE FALLEN

One of the most controversial shrines in the world, General Franco's rival to the Escorial is just a few miles away. The Valley of the Fallen is a Civil War memorial, presumably a peace symbol for both sides, for the dead of both may be buried there. It is, of course, harshly criticized by both sides: by friends of Franco because he tolerates his adversaries; by the latter because of its association with him. It is also criticized for its cost. No one knows how many millions of pesetas and of man-hours (it is darkly said that forced labor did most of it) went into this gigantic crypt, blasted nearly nine hundred feet right into the solid granite and mounted by a five hundred-foot-high cross.

Before visiting the Valley of the Fallen I was repelled by the thought of it, and almost avoided it altogether. It reminded me too much of the Pyramids and other monuments where men's labor was horribly misused. However, the visit is surely worthwhile, and whether or not you like the memorial, you will be inspired to pray for Spain, and for the victims of the Civil War, and all war victims, and for peace. You will also agree that it is easily the most imposing of modern monuments.

TOLEDO

There is a single city which can serve as the microcosm of Spain, which you should visit above all others if you wish to savor Spain in all its variety. That city is Toledo. For second choice, there would be little agreement. Would it be Avila, Segovia, Seville, Santiago, Granada?

The guidebooks will offer you opposing views about seeing Toledo. Some say not to go if you have only a day. That, to me, is snobbery verging on masochism. My first visit had to be limited to one day, a day which I number among the most memorable of my life. Give Toledo a day, a week, a month, and you will be as delighted that you went as reluctant to leave.

To prepare yourself, see El Greco's painting of the city in New York's Metropolitan, and don't be pedantically disturbed over the license he took in redistributing the landscape for his artistic purposes.

In Toledo the one thing that will disappoint you is the renovated Alcázar. Don't bother to spend much time there, but go rather to the cathedral—said to be the largest Gothic structure in the world (as though that mattered; besides is it really Gothic?).

The cathedral, with its sprawling, rich imaginativeness, will remind you not only of Spain but of the whole Church. Unlike Notre-Dame de Paris, with its tight, austere, logical structure, Toledo's cathedral goes off in all directions, all of them impressive and human. The liturgy is, of course, in the Roman rite, but the feeling is so Spanish that you may wonder what rite it is. You will be reminded that Catholicism means unity, not uniformity, and you will not resent the fine feeling of diversity within wholeness. This impression is accentuated by the presence of a chapel within the cathedral where the liturgy is, even today, performed in a non-Roman rite—the Mozarabic—which goes back to pre-Moslem-conquest times, when the Church in Spain had a strong Visigothic flavor. Cardinal Ximenes preserved the ancient usage, and every day you may participate in an ancient Catholic and Western liturgy that is not Roman. Wonderful symbol of the Church Catholic.

Artistically too the cathedral is one of the world's great shrines. The paintings in the sacristy alone make it a major museum, where you may see El Greco's compassionate "Espolio," a set of portraits of the Apostles (there is another set in his house, which you must see too), and masterpieces of Velázquez, Goya, Raphael, Titian, Rubens and others. Twenty-five of the stalls were the work of one of the world's great sculptors, Berruguete, and Pedro de Mena's statue of St. Francis seems to me one of the supreme pieces of sacred sculpture in the world, almost modern in its leanness and simplicity. The list of treasures could go on and on.

You will not miss El Greco's home, nor the Church of Santo Tomé with what is probably his masterpiece, the "Burial of Count Orgaz" (beautifully illumined now and seen to best advantage). But, to me personally, one of the most haunting memories of Toledo is that of the two main former synagogues: Del Tránsito and Santa María la Blanca. We all have some idea of the heartless expulsion of the Jews from Spain in the fifteenth century. What is not so well known is that for some four centuries before this, the Jewish community in Spain was extremely vigorous and enjoyed a golden age. Moses Maimonides (1135-1204) was by no means the only eminent Spanish-Jewish thinker to achieve world stature. Here in Toledo, the heart of Christian Spain, the Jews were particularly creative, and the exquisite workmanship seen in these two synagogues, with texts from Holy Scripture adorning the walls, is a heart-rending reminder of Spain's loss.

Amid the treasures of this city, which itself is a vast treasury, you may have the time and energy to visit a former mosque, now a church called Cristo de la Luz ("Christ of the Light"). It is so called because, all through the years of Moslem control (Toledo was retaken in 1085), the Christians kept a vigil light burning before a hidden image of Christ beneath the mosque. Another shrine,

in a totally different style, is the monastery of San
Juan de los Reyes. "Reyes"("Kings") in Spain
always refers to "Los Reyes Católicos"—Ferdinand and Isabella. The building is a model
of the Spanish Gothic-Renaissance manner known
as "plateresque," and in its own way is very moving.

For more painting, if you are not prostrate by
now, you may visit the Hospital de San Juan
Bautista ("St. John the Baptist") built by El
Greco's son, with its many works by El Greco,
Titian, Tintoretto and others; and the museum of
San Vincente, where you may see, side by side,
paintings by El Greco and their imitations by
Velázquez. A fascinating and rare experience.
And, finally, you will want to visit a number of
shops where the tradition of metal craftsmanship
has been kept alive—a good place to purchase
gifts.

You will not want to leave this ancient capital,
sacred and civil, where the Church was holding
important councils back in the fourth century, a
city which has been through all the joys and sor-
rows of Western civilization.

AVILA

So photogenic is Avila, for all the bleakness of
the surrounding country, that everyone must know
its walls and crenelations. It was only natural that
a movie should be made in and around it. But,
apart from the picturesque battlements—or rather,

perhaps symbolized by them—is the great spiritual power generated by two Carmelite saints, St. Teresa and St. John of the Cross. (He was not from Avila but is closely associated with Teresa and Avila.) St. John has been given the supreme accolade of "Doctor of the Church"; but since that title has been unexplainably reserved only for masculine saints (I can think of some explanations, but feel they should be left discreetly unsaid), St. Teresa is simply St. Teresa, Virgin (not Doctor). A few years ago, the faculty of Salamanca, in a burst of feminist gallantry, did its best to make up for the slight: on the walls of the University you will see a diploma of Doctor of Sacred Theology awarded (*in absentia* and posthumously) to Teresa of Avila. No one could deserve it more. Apart from the Blessed Virgin—Seat of Wisdom—and possibly St. Joan of Arc, is she not the greatest woman in history?

You will surely want to visit her house and assist at the Holy Sacrifice in her rooms. It is one of the great shrines of Christendom, where one senses the power of prayer and contemplation. The cathedral too, though small, is not to be forgotten. It seems part of the great walls, like one of their eighty-eight towers. As you walk around the city you will also pay a visit to the shrine of St. Vincent and his disciples, Sts. Sabina and Cristeta, in the handsome church named after him. But greater than any single building is Avila itself, the highest city in all Spain, and, its inhabitants say, the closest to heaven.

SEGOVIA

Near Avila, and in some ways even more picturesque, is ancient Segovia, considered, like Toledo and Santiago, a national monument. The
three most conspicuous monuments are the cathedral, the Alcázar and the aqueduct. For some
two thousand years, the ancient Roman aqueduct
carried water to the city; today it simply stands
there, a symbol of continuity and a reminder of
how well and how far the Romans built. Ninety
feet high in one section, and nine hundred feet
across the city's ravine, it is one of the most imposing of Roman monuments anywhere. (With
considerable reluctance, I shall not have space to
treat of Tarragona, where even more monuments
are in evidence.)

The Alcázar is, in the popular image, *the* castle
of Spain, and possibly for that reason Walt Disney
used it as a model in his *Snow White and the
Seven Dwarfs*. It was from here that Queen Isabella rode out to be crowned. There are, of course,
a number of other romantic details to the history
of this towering structure. Below, you will want to
see the church of the Knights Templar, the Vera
Cruz; but it will be hard to draw the line amid so
many venerable churches.

Save some of your psychic and spiritual energy
for the cathedral. As Chartres is called the Queen
of French Cathedrals, the great church of Segovia
is known as the Lady of Spanish Cathedrals. It

is late Gothic, with an immense tiled cupola. Like
Salamanca's cathedral it seems all golden. Within,
you will be impressed and charmed by the treasured paintings and by the holiness that seems to
pervade the building itself.

If you crave something more worldly, La
Granja, a sort of miniature Versailles, is just a few
miles from Segovia. Its gardens and tapestries
designed by Goya, though almost trivial compared
to Segovia itself, are treasures of another sort.

SALAMANCA

Salamanca, the golden city, tends to be bypassed
by pilgrims, perhaps because it is not on any main
line of traffic. Yet, to me and to many it seems
the handsomest of university towns (and I say this
with all deference to Oxford, Cambridge and
Coimbra), despite the havoc suffered under the
Moslems and later, Napoleon, Spain's great de-
stroyer. Like Toledo, it was reconquered in 1085.
In the later Middle Ages and Renaissance the
university ranked with the finest in the world. The
Spanish have a proverb about Salamanca: "What
God does not give, Salamanca doesn't either"—a
healthy reminder that not even such a university
can remedy IQ deficiency.

The two cathedrals (both Catholic—not like
London or New York or other pluralistic cities!)
are among the great ones of Spain: the old one
with walls like battlements, the new one more

graceful. There are elegant mansions, not least the House of the Shells, which seems to be included in all works on architecture, and across the street from it, the Jesuit Church of the Clerecía. But the city as a whole is a treasurehouse, full of rich memories of saints, scholars and scholar-saints. One of the most beautiful single architectural gems is the portal of the university, a superb example of plateresque (an ornamental style, derived from the silversmith technique, "platero"). One of the greatest and least known of Spanish paintings is hidden away in a convent chapel of the Augustines —"The Immaculate Conception" by Ribera, which I find more moving than Murillo's treatments of the subject.

SANTIAGO DE COMPOSTELA

The patron saint of Spain, whether or not he ever set foot on the peninsula, is St. James the Greater, the Apostle. During the Middle Ages when pilgrimages were widely used as a means toward sanctification, his shrine at Compostela rivaled Rome and Jerusalem. "Santiago," of course, means St. James. History, in a sense, seems to matter less here than elsewhere. It is impossible to prove—or disprove—that St. James was ever here, though there is evidence of graves dating back to apostolic times. In any case, it has been made a holy place by centuries and centuries of prayer on the part of many millions of pilgrims.

The Spanish call the Milky Way "El Camino de Santiago"—so much is it like the path of countless pilgrim candles to Compostela.

The cathedral itself is a gem of twelfth-century architecture, with a rich overlay of plateresque and baroque. If you want your architecture to be consistently functional and no more, you will be unhappy in Spain, and perhaps unhappiest of all in Santiago. (But why be unhappy?)

Cathedrals, and especially shrines, are best seen when in full use; the best time to see this wondrous place is on some great feast, such as the Assumption. You will hardly believe your eyes, even forewarned, when you see a gigantic incense burner swinging hundreds of feet overhead, through what has been calculated as a 260-foot arc. It is called the "Botafumeiro."

The entire city is treasured by the nation as a whole, and is protected as a national monument. Any changes or additions must be approved by a special committee in charge of Spain's treasures. Thus, the ancient atmosphere, one conducive to pilgrimage, is preserved. Walk slowly around the whole city, view the unbelievable façade of the cathedral (the "Obradoiro"), and pray at the spot where millions of other pilgrims have prayed over the years, and you will find Santiago unique in that unique land. Don't be too surprised if you hear a Spanish that doesn't sound like Spanish; the language of Galicia is closer to Portuguese than to Castilian. The climate, the mist and almost incessant drizzle, and the bagpipes (if you get to hear them) will remind you too that Gael and Galicia have a great deal in common. Another of Spain's surprises.

BARCELONA

Spain's second city, Barcelona, is perhaps the most surprising spot in that land of surprises. Were you to land by helicopter right on the Gran Via or in the midst of the Plaza de Cataluña you could easily believe you were in Paris. Listen to the people talk, and you hear a language that is obviously not Spanish. Is it French? you wonder, noting the crisp, consonantal pronunciation.

Catalan, the language of Catalonia, is quite as much a language as French or Spanish, and has something in common with both. But, please, don't call it a dialect of either. It is a highly literary, independent tongue, the official language of the Catalonian and Aragonese monarchy. Documents in Catalan date back to the eleventh century. Ramón Lull (c. 1233-c. 1315) was a major poet and the first philosopher to use a Romance language; his tongue was Catalan. Today there is a great renaissance in Catalan literature, and, though the government at Madrid tries to restrict its use severely (it is feared as a symbol of separatism), the language is spoken by some eight million people. You may want to try your hand at reading it, if you know Spanish or Italian. The effort will charm and exasperate you.

The people of Barcelona will amaze you. They

are sophisticated and industrious like the French, but as animated as the Spanish. If you have a chance to meet their intellectuals, again you will be reminded of Paris. Some of the most vigorous Christian thought of our time goes on in Barcelona and its neighborhood. Among writers, the great novelist José María Gironella (author of *The Cypresses Believe in God* and *A Million Dead*) lives part of the time in Barcelona, part in his native Gerona (where the action of *The Cypresses* is placed), and part in a lovely coast town to the north, Arenys de Mar, where one of the most attractive little churches of the area is to be found. If you have time and a car, you will do well to drive up the coast, the famous Costa Brava, Spain's Riviera.

Barcelona has everything. If you want to see the Roman city, parts of it you can find preserved near the cathedral. There are even vestiges of the pre-Roman Greek city. Barcelona was also a Carthaginian city, an Arab one, a Visigothic one too. What is called the Barrio Gótico ("Gothic Quarter") will very likely prove most interesting, close as it is to the great medieval cathedral, with its shrines of holiness and Christian art.

More spectacular than the cathedral is the world-famous church of the Sagrada Familia ("Holy Family"), the unfinished masterpiece of Barcelona's renowned architect Gaudí. Do see it, and you will agree that no adjective (at least not in English, Catalan may have one) can be fittingly applied to it. It is more than fantastic, phantasmagoric, outrageous—more and less. In fact, if you are interested in modern architecture and some of its more amazing vagaries, see everything done by Gaudí. Most of his work is in Barcelona.

Try to be there on a week end. The great convent of Pedralbes contains the art of a master almost as original as Giotto himself, Ferrer Bassá. Almost all of his extant work is in one little room of the convent, and it can be seen only on Sundays, for a few hours. Prepare yourself by reading about Bassá in the Skira volume *Spanish Painting*. And in the same volume, learn all you can about Bartolomé Bermejo, another great master whose work is largely in Barcelona.

Another reason to be in Barcelona on a week end is to see the great fountain that plays on Saturday and Sunday nights, at the foot of Montjuich. If there is another fountain in the world to be mentioned in the same breath as this, I have neither seen nor heard of it. Thousands of jets, with as many lights, play in a symphony of moving forms—abstract art at its most appealing. Experts say that, week end after week end, over a period of years, the symphonic score has never been repeated.

Possibly Barcelona's greatest artistic glory, at least for the history-minded, is to be found at the top of Montjuich in the Palacio Nacional. There the museum of Catalan art contains the most comprehensive collection of Romanesque painting in the world. In Boston we have one chapel, laboriously brought over from Spain, with a remarkable collection of frescoes of the Romanesque period; and in the Cloisters in New York we have another chapel, with an impressive apse, also in the same style. But the Palacio Nacional houses literally hundreds of sacred masterpieces.

Near the Palacio you may care to relax by seeing a miniature of all Spain, the Pueblo Español exhibition. There you will find the infinite variety of the country illumined, all its regions and principal cities with streets and buildings in replica.

The great shrine of the Sacred Heart, called the "Tibidabo," is worth a visit for several reasons. One is the superb view of the Mediterranean of Barcelona as a whole, which looks, as someone said, "at sunset like a shining city buried in the sea."

MONTSERRAT

Few cities even in Europe offer the diverse scope of interest that you will find in Barcelona, but exceptional as a pilgrimage site is nearby Montserrat. You may go by car or bus, but simplest and safest is the train trip, starting in the Plaza de España. You wander through the factory-studded suburbs of what may be the most industrialized city on the Mediterranean, through one of the greenest areas in parched Spain; then suddenly you spot a mountain that seems like a scene from Wagner.

Indeed, when Wagner glimpsed the awesome mountain (I was told he only glimpsed it), he quite naturally thought of it as the appropriate shrine for the Holy Grail. Montsalvat, he calls it in *Parsifal,* to suggest the Mountain of Salvation. Montserrat actually means Sawtooth Mountain.

Rising, almost without warning, out of the plain, thousands of feet into the air, high and aloof, it was naturally thought of as a holy place. From time immemorial it has been so reckoned. And from at least the ninth century it has been a hermitage, where the "Black Madonna" ("La Moreneta," as she is called in Catalan) is cherished. She is one of the best beloved of Our Lady's images. One thinks immediately of the texts (mistranslations, but now traditional): "I am black but beautiful" and "All the beauty of the King's daughter is from within," for the statue is squat and ungainly, anything but superficially lovely.

During the eleventh century, the Abbot Oliva of Ripoll arrived with a group of monks, and from that day Montserrat has been a great center of worship.

Though the present building is not really ancient (Napoleon's soldiers, who destroyed so much of Spain's architectural glory, destroyed the old monastery), it is imposing. The abbey church is spacious and open and hospitable. The monks are seated in their stalls around the apse, behind the altar, facing outward toward the people. You will feel, at Mass, that you belong and are not merely a spectator.

Be sure to be there at least for the daily Solemn Mass. In few places that I know do you receive such a feeling of participation, of social worship (which, of course, is what "liturgy" means). The singing too is worthy. Montserrat's monks form one of the great monastic choirs of the world. Moreover, the monastery encloses what is known as the oldest music school in Europe, the Escolanía, where young boys come to study music and other subjects. The boys' choir is trained by Father Ireneu Segarra, who insists that they learn theory and two instruments in addition to singing.

The boys (who have made some delightful records, by the way) sing on important occasions, but you can hear them every afternoon, right after lunch, at a special little service, the "Salve" in honor of Our Lady of Montserrat. They gather below her shrine and sing the "Hail, Holy Queen," using a different musical version each day of the week. It is an experience not likely to be forgotten. As you admire these young boys, you wonder how many of them will become leaders in the world of music, like Antoni Soler, Ferran Sor and other masters who one day studied there on the mountain of music. (One of the boys now in the choir is named, coincidentally, Pablo Casals.)

Montserrat has been visited by millions of fervent Christians. In the abbey church is an unusual tablet containing the names of canonized saints who once made the pilgrimage there. No case is perhaps more celebrated than that of young Iñigo de Loyola (not yet "St. Ignatius"), who following his wounding at the Battle of Pamplona in 1521 and a long painful convalescence in his castle at Loyola, made the arduous journey across the north of Spain and up the mountain. One wonders how anyone could make it on foot, and then one remembers that Iñigo had barely recovered from a serious leg wound. There, near the "Moreneta," he made his knightly vigil, (March 25, 1522) vowing himself henceforth to be a knight of the Kingdom of God. Accordingly, in this majestic Benedictine monastery there is considerable devotion to St. Ignatius and even an altar dedicated to his memory.

MANRESA

At the foot of Montserrat, along the rivers Llobregat and Cardoner, is a not-too-prepossessing town called Manresa. In a cave near here the *Spiritual Exercises* of St. Ignatius de Loyola struggled into being. Here he wrestled with powers and principalities as the full meaning of the Gospels was revealed to him. In time, he organized these "exercises" into the form in which they are presented to millions of serious Christians in search of God's purpose. The name of Manresa is known to thousands of American men as a haven of stillness where, in retreat, one may most intimately commune with God.

Manresa has thus become a shrine, not only to Jesuits, but to all who have made the *Spiritual Exercises*. Years later, Ignatius referred to this cave as his blessed "primitive church." It was while walking along the banks of the nearby

Cardoner that he experienced a transforming mystical illumination. In his own words: "It was not that he actually beheld some vision but rather there was given to him a knowledge and understanding of many things of the spiritual life . . . so brilliant an enlightenment that everything appeared new . . . a wonderful clarity." Father Nadal, one of his confidants, asserted that it was here that God "led him to give himself completely to His service and the welfare of souls."

Above the cave in which Ignatius prayed has been built an immense retreat house, prototype of so many others, called Manresa. The cave itself has been unpleasantly cluttered up—such is the fate of so many shrines—with well-intended ornaments, and only the native rock of the ceiling shows it as Ignatius knew it. But it remains a holy place, where one enjoys praying in union with the Saint of Generosity.

LOYOLA CASTLE

There are as many "Loyolas" as "Manresas" in America, and "Loyola" alumni now number in the millions. At this point, accordingly, I shall say a word about the original Loyola, which, though not near Manresa in any geographical sense, is its spiritual neighbor.

Of the great shrines associated with saints and founders of religious movements, few can be less appealing than Loyola. Like Ignatius himself, who became the most modest and unassuming of

men, effacing himself behind his work—or rather
God's work—Loyola has little surface charm.
Nor is it on any beaten track. However, if you
are in Bilbao, San Sebastian, or Burgos, it is not
at all complicated to catch a train to Azpeitia
and Azcoitia, where the Loyola castle is.

The castle proper has been smothered by later
architecture, enclosed in a pretentious basilica
within the buildings of the Jesuit novitiate. What
attracts the pilgrim, however, is the room where
Ignatius was converted during his convalescence.
It is on the top story; through the windows Ignatius could see Mt. Izarraitz toward the north. The
sickroom has been turned appropriately into a
chapel, where the pilgrim may have the privilege
of offering the Holy Sacrifice. On the ancient
wooden beam overhead are the simple words:
"Here Iñigo de Loyola gave himself to God."
They are eloquent enough.

SEVILLE

Few cities anywhere have been so entrancing to
visitors as Seville. Indeed, the image that flashes
before the stranger's mind as he hears the word
"Spain" is likely to be tinted with the colors of
Seville and of Andalusia generally. Seville was
famous before Rome existed, and its charm shows
no signs of exhaustion. The Guadalquivir, on
which it stands, is Arabic for the river the Romans
called the Betis—hence the province of Betica and
the excellent football team (Seville's "Giants")

called, quite simply, "the Betis." Don't be too surprised at all the names that begin with *Guad* —the Arabic for "river": Guadarama, Guadalajara, Guadalupe, Guadalcanal. They will help remind you that for about seven centuries the South of Spain (and much besides) was under Arab control.

This part of Spain is, in some ways, the least European, the most Euro-African. Many of the people look as if they had Arab blood, and they probably do. More than blood has survived— much of the music, styles of dance, architecture, ways of living are Arab in inspiration. Your first view of Seville from the plane or train or car will be the graceful Giralda, once part of the principal mosque, now the tower of the cathedral. (You'll find it a strenuous climb, especially if you are overweight, but the view from the top is unforgettable.)

The cathedral itself, of course, is one of the world's wonders, not only in size but in treasure. The great retable of the high altar is awe-inspiring. (I suggest that you try *not* to be there when the canons sing; at least the times I have heard them chant the divine office or High Mass, I thought it the worst music in all Christendom.) Columbus' massive tomb—whether or not his body is still there is a moot point; he can claim tombs elsewhere—is worth a few moments of contemplation.

You will want to spend some time in the Alcázar, one of the supreme works of Arab art, and in the gardens. And, by all means, see the Hospital de la Caridad, built by Don Miguel de Mañara, who is said to be the inspiration for the various Don Juan legends. (The Don lead an exemplary life as a religious after his conversion.) Murillo, a native Sevillian, spent an entire year adorning the inspiring chapel. Velázquez was another great Sevillian painter, who, though he is represented in the museum, Spain's third best, must be seen in the Prado to be known at all.

The wonder of Holy Week in Seville is, of course, proverbial. It is devotional, social, entertaining and a display of fabulous art all at the same time. To see the great statues carried in the processions is alone worth the trouble of facing the crowds. For Spanish sculpture to match this, you will have to go to Valladolid. (I hope you do, but we shall not have space to guide you there.)

Unique to Seville are "Los Seises," a choir of children, with special garb, who are allowed to dance in the cathedral before the Blessed Sacrament. To see them, you will have to be there at the feasts of the Immaculate Conception and Corpus Christi. If dance too is an art, why should it not sing the glory of God?

One more word about Seville as a shrine. St. Isidore of Seville may be only a name in the religious calendar to you, but if you review your history you will find him as perhaps the most learned man in the Western world around the year 600. He is described as the link between the scholarship of antiquity and that of the Middle Ages. Bishop St. Leander, too, is venerated here, and throughout

Spain is considered a Doctor of the Church. If you have time, drive out to see the ruins of Italica, another great Roman city, where the emperors Trajan and Hadrian were born. It once boasted a coliseum of forty thousand seats.

CORDOVA

It is hard for us to realize that when London and Paris were only towns, and Rome had fallen from its eminence, Cordova was the cultural and intellectual capital of the West. Its libraries were said to contain four hundred thousand volumes, at a period when books were exceedingly rare. Here was the home of great Arab and Jewish philosophers, men like Averroës, Maimonides, Avicebron. Even earlier, in Roman days, the two Senecas and their relative, the poet Lucan, came from Cordova. There seems a touch of the Senecas—those worthy Stoics—in today's Cordovans, with their dignity and austere aristocracy. Modern Cordova produced the matador of matadors, the great Manolete. A handsome monument honors the hero.

The greatest building in Cordova is, as commonly in Spain, the cathedral. You will be surprised at its location: right in the middle of the immense mosque, "La Mesquita." Before you shudder in horror at what Charles V ordered done to the mosque, you may want to remember that it too occupies the site and much of the actual materials of an earlier cathedral built by the Christian Visigoths. The lines of monolithic columns—many hundreds of them—produce an effect unlike that of any building I know. These 850 columns have been described as a "marble forest," and Christian or Moslem, they suggest an atmosphere of prayer. One afternoon, when the mosque was closed for the unavoidable siesta, I managed to stay inside alone. The great *mihrab,* sacred spot where the Koran was reserved, adorned with most precious arabesques and mosaics, attracted me and proved an appropriate and easy place to meditate. Surely the centuries of prayer that have gone up from the mosque-cathedral have not been in vain. You will be impressed by the mighty inscription: *Christus vincit, Christus regnat, Christus imperat* ("Christ conquers, Christ reigns, Christ commands").

Another holy place in Cordova is the synagogue, where during the Middle Ages Jews prayed in peace amid Moslems and Christians. The surrounding area is still called the Judería, or Jewish Quarter. I asked a young boy if there were any Jews living there, and he hardly understood my question. He had never known a Jew. I asked about the Arabs. That question surprised him too. Yet his face seemed to say that his ancestors had been Arabs.

Cordova's patron is St. Raphael, and the lively Sevillians enjoy twitting their neighbors about him. The Sevillians say that the Cordovans claim to have a feather from St. Raphael's angelic wings. The jest is not appreciated in Cordova, but this is not to say that the city has no lighter side.

Just outside the city, you may want to see Las Hermitas—one of the few real hermitages in the Western world, where men live the lives of the ancient desert monastics. Their hermitage may be visited, up in the nearby mountain. Next to it, if you prefer something more conventional, is the new Jesuit novitiate.

GRANADA

The third of Andalusian cities, and in some ways the most famous of all, is also the most Arab. The Granadinos even look Arab. Music seems in the air; a famous composer spoke of the very landscape as the most "musical" of Europe. The Alhambra, called "the rarest piece of architecture in the West," defies description. Yet few buildings have been more often described (remember Washington Irving, whose rooms are there) or more stunningly photographed. To catch your breath amid such dazzling elegance, be sure to look out over the valley and capture Granada as a whole. Then walk slowly through the incomparable Generalife gardens. You may feel, after this, that the civilization that produced such works had reached the point where decadence set in. Perhaps we are only reading history backwards, with our prejudices.

It was the capture of Granada that ended the Arab sway in Spain—1492 is important for two events in Spanish history. Ferdinand and Isabella are buried in this city of their conquest. Austerely leaden are their coffins, within the sumptuous monument in the cathedral.

One of Granada's principal shrines is the Charterhouse or Cartuja, a treasury of baroque splendor hard to equal anywhere, even in Spain. Prepare to be overpowered.

Finally, if you want to be a really typical tourist, you may visit some of Granada's gypsies, in the nearby caves of Monte Sacro. They seem made to order, perhaps too good to be true, everything a tourist wants. Their caves, I am told, have the modern necessities—radio, telephone, and, as soon as television is available, that too, in all probability.

OTHER PLACES OF INTEREST

No chapter can do justice to Spain. I hope you have time to move up and down from Santiago, to Vigo, to La Guardia, to Mount Tecla, and down to Caminha across the Minho to Portugal. Still more, I hope you find a way to visit Valladolid, not too far from Salamanca, with its incomparable sculpture in wood and several superb cloisters, especially San Gregorio. Valladolid was once a capital of Spain. And León, another capital, with what some consider the finest of Spanish cathedrals. And then **Burgos,** capital of Old Castile, home of El Cid, his burial place is in the splendid cathedral—the most Gothic of all those of Spain—Burgos with the Cartuja de Miraflores and nearby monastery of Silos, where you will hear Solesmes-like chant and see authentic Romanesque sculpture in abundance. And farther north, Santillana del Mar, as medieval as Assisi. Then be sure not to miss Spain's oldest treasure, often called the "Sistine of the Paleolithic age" —the great caves of **Altamira** near Santander. The story of how these paleolithic paintings were discovered need not now be retold. But here, more I believe than anywhere, one senses the misery and glory of man, observing paintings that go back some twenty or forty thousand years, paintings that were ancient and forgotten when the pyramids of Egypt were not yet built, that date back to an era before mankind discovered agriculture or learned to domesticate animals. Altamira too is a holy place, a shrine, where our pre-prehistoric ancestors tried somehow to come into communion with something above themselves, and where, without too much imagination, we can feel something in common with them.

I have not mentioned the sanctuary of Nuestra Señora del Pilar at Saragossa, or of Aránzazu, or La Rábida, or Guadalupe (of Spain, not Mexico), or Poblet (where the kings of Aragon are buried in dignity and some splendor), or Covadonga (where the Reconquista began), or Nuestra Señora de la Cabeza in Sierra Morena, or Vich or a hundred other spots of Catalonia, or Urgel in the Basque country, or Valencia in the Garden of Spain (famed for its association with El Cid, for natural beauty and for its claim to the Holy Grail). Nor have I spoken of Peñíscola (where Benedict

XIII was pope, so he thought, over a part of Christendom during the terrible schism), or Elche (where was found the famed statue, "La Dama de Elche" dating back at least ten centuries before Christ), or Aranjuez, or Málaga, or Cádiz, or Jérez . . . But where does one stop in inexhaustible Spain?

PORTUGAL

"Here in this small land of Portugal there will not be wanting men to do and dare for Christendom . . . If Spain is the head of Europe, Portugal is the crown on the head!" So sang Camoëns, the Homer and Virgil of Portugal, in ringing words memorized by every Portuguese schoolboy for some four centuries.

The first and most relevant thing to remember about Portugal, especially if you arrive there after your Spanish visit, is that it is not Spain, nor any part thereof, any more than Ireland is England or Canada the United States. Rather, if could be, less so.

For example, if you expect to understand the Portuguese when they speak, and you only have some college Spanish, you will be almost as bewildered as if you were trying to untangle Swahili. Yet, you may be able to get the Portuguese to understand you as you stumble along in the tongue of Cervantes. For to them, Spanish sounds like a simplified Portuguese, rather unsubtle but intelligible—a "pidgin Portuguese." Indeed, Portuguese uses many more sounds than Spanish (I gave up after counting at least ten vowels unknown to Spanish, before embarking on the sea of Portuguese nasals). When you first encounter the language, you will find it as elusive, and perhaps more subtle even than French.

However, linguistic differences between Portugal and Spain are perhaps the least profound. Take bullfights, for example. They differ, you will discover, in just about everything except the fact that bulls are involved. The fighters, in Portugal, ride on horseback; the bull's horns are padded to save the horse from harm; the matador does not kill the bull, but only goes through a symbolic act of vanquishing him.

Name almost any trait that you reckon typically Spanish, and you will find it as typically un-Portuguese. Every trait, I should have said, except dignity, courtesy and a certain proud disdain for mere speed. And when you enter Lisbon for the first time, you will do well to divest yourself of all the clichés you have heard about Portugal. For, while the country is distressingly poor, the capital is one of the most elegant in the world.

LISBON

The streets are graceful and tree-lined. Lisbon's subway (there is a subway—not a long one, and not a very useful one; but it is there) glides gently and almost noiselessly between stations adorned with tasteful mosaic and tile work. A city ordinance, too, requires the fronts of all buildings to be repainted at least once every seven years. Thus, in colorfulness and a scrubbed look, few cities can rival Lisbon; for, though northern cities tend to excel in neatness and southern cities in color, few anywhere, except possibly San Francisco, reconcile both virtues.

To grasp Lisbon's unique loveliness, see it from the other side of the Mar de Palha ("Sea of Straw"), which is the broad estuary of the Tagus. (You may have trouble recognizing this majestic, blue body of water as the same Tagus that struggles around Toledo, many miles upstream in parched Castile.) From the gigantic new statue of Christ, there is an unforgettable vista, especially at twilight, when the city begins to sparkle. But any time of day or night will do, for Lisbon's beauty is inherent, not conditioned by a romantic moment, when almost any city assumes some charm. Once more you will think of San Francisco.

Again, like its Pacific counterpart, Lisbon suffered hideously from an earthquake, which brought its destruction and resurrection. In 1755, on All Saints' day, the tragic event took place while thousands were in church—a calamity much publicized and exploited cynically by Voltaire in his *Candide*. Not many significant ancient buildings were left standing, though you will see an occasional Gothic arch as a pitiful reminder.

Some churches remain and are worth a visit. There is the **Sé** or cathedral. In the former refectory of the great church of St. Vincent, Lisbon's patron, you will see the tombs of rulers of Portugal's royal house of Braganza. In this "Pantheon," as it is called, you will find the tomb of King Carol of Rumania, who died in exile and was given posthumous hospitality amid his peers. The Church of St. Roque, too, contains graves of famous men, among them the theologian Suarez.

But far surpassing anything to be found in Lisbon for national tradition and architectural splendor is the church called the **Jeronimos** (named after the Jeronimite or Hieronymite Fathers, whose monastic church it was). Unlike any Gothic structure you have seen elsewhere, even in Spain, its exotic ornaments and arabesques and unusual lighting make you feel you are in a mysterious grotto. The style, peculiar to Portugal, is called Manueline, after Manuel I (1495-1520), under whom the Portuguese empire spread over what was known of the world. Combining a number of sea-faring motifs with palms, tropical plants, seaweed, even elephant tusks, it recalls Portugal's exploits on many seas. Along with the vast church, there is a cloister in the same exuberant style, and not far away, the famous tower of Belem. It was from Belem, the former Restello, that Vasco da Gama set forth to discover a sea route to India. The Jeronimos is an immortal monument to his memory.

Toward the main entrance of the church, you will notice two honored tombs: one is Vasco da Gama's; the other belongs to Portugal's great poet, Luiz de Camoëns, who celebrated da Gama's exploits and those of all the Portuguese. The *Lusiads,* the national epic, is well worth reading,

if need be in translation. Through all the hyperbole, rhetoric and twisted history you will feel
something of the grandeur and glory that were
Portugal's. The Lusiads (sons of Lusus, Portugal's legendary founder) are the Portuguese themselves, and they honor their national poet by an
annual holiday, "Camoëns' Day." This is some
recompense for the knowledge that Camoëns died
penniless and his actual burial place is unknown.
Yet, despite natural rivalries, the greatest Spanish
writers—Cervantes, Lope de Vega, Calderón and
others—speak of Camoëns with awe, as someone
greater than themselves.

Thus, the Jeronimos is more than a national
monument. It is the symbol of an epic period,
when gallant men sailed forth from here to discover and conquer a world. Colonialism is, of
course, an anachronism and a dirty word today.
Yet, if the world is today moving toward oneness,
however haltingly, much of its progress may be
credited to these Lusiads, who quite consciously,
if obliquely and not altogether unselfishly, strove
to make it one. "Let us hear no more of Ulysses
and Aeneas and their long journeyings," sang
Camoëns, "no more of Alexander and Trajan and
their famous victories. The heroes and poets of
old have had their day. Another and loftier conception of valor has arisen. My theme is the dar-
ing and renown of the Portuguese." There is
irony and a good deal of pathos in these thrilling
words.

Quite near the Jeronimos is the strange but famed Museum of Coaches. By no means as frivolous as one would think, it is worth a brief visit, if only as a vivid study in contrasting national and social traditions. If the car is something of a status symbol to us today, how much more so were the non-mass-produced carriages of popes and kings and nobility. A very bizarre collection this is, but one that affords surprising insights into such diverse personalities as, say, Philip II of Spain and Louis XIV of France.

Like any capital, Lisbon possesses many other museums, but you may bypass most of them with little loss. One exception is the Museum of Ancient Art, where you will find a representative collection of Portugal's greatest painter, Nuño Gonçalves, and of several Dutch, Spanish and Italian masters. To me, the most exciting painting here is a triptych by Hieronymus Bosch—his fierce "Temptation of St. Anthony."

Lisbon boasts another St. Anthony, not the Anthony of the "Temptation" but the saint whom the Italians like to call "St. Anthony of Padua." He is the beloved patron of the Portuguese. The wittiest sermon I ever heard or read was about him. The work of Father Antonio Vieira, Portugal's leading orator and possibly her greatest *prosateur,* it treats of St. Anthony preaching to the fishes. The sermon deals with Christian social teaching, as Father Vieira piquantly compares the saint's listeners to fish in their fondness for devouring each other and makes other pointed admonitions needed by his sophisticated audience, the privileged class of the seventeenth century.

Another beloved saint of the Lisboetas (Lisbonese) is John de Britto, one of numberless missioners who sailed out of their harbor to gather souls for Christ. St. John was "ahead of his times," in his missionary technique. Adapting to local cultures is deemed by modern students to have been the right apostolic approach. Had his policy of adaptation been followed, it is conceivable, they believe, that all India, not just a few million Indians, would today be Christian. If you do find St. John's birthplace, you may be surprised, as I was, to discover it in what is now a bar—an exceptional spot for a shrine. Still another eminent missioner, often called the greatest since the days of the Apostles, also set out from Lisbon under Portuguese auspices. This was, of course, St. Francis Xavier.

Following the earthquake, Lisbon was superbly rebuilt in the style of the period. The Praça do Comércio ("Place of Commerce"), down near the river and once the center of the city, is a gem among city squares. In our country, the only comparable plaza is New Orleans' Place d'Armes (called by the Spanish the "Plaza de Armas" and in English "Jackson Square"), built at roughly the same period in a similar geographical site. But the Mississippi is hidden behind levees and warehouses, whereas the Tagus lies fair and open to view.

Indeed, Lisbon and its harbor offer an almost unparalleled variety of vistas—from the castle, from the Edward VII Garden, from any of the *miradouros* ("viewing spots"), especially from the one called Santa Luzia. But for atmosphere, stroll around at leisure in the Alfama quarter, or around the Praça do Rocio ("Place of the Rock"), stopping at any of the coffee shops nearby. One of the most illustrious of these is Nicola's, where writers and journalists like to gather and talk endlessly in lieu of reading a free press, a place immortalized in verses by the Romantic poet Bocage. But unless you are a man, you will feel out of place there. Coffee shops are strictly a man's world.

THE ENVIRONS

In the vicinity of Lisbon, too, there is a great deal to attract the tourist. When you see the pleasant resort of Estoril, you will not wonder why many of Europe's exiled royalty or nobility (including Spain's Don Juan Carlos) chose this as a place to live and entertain each other. To the north is Sintra, a spot of fantastic loveliness, with an ancient Moorish castle and one of the most interesting palaces in Portugal. Nazaré, on the ocean, is filled with atmosphere and is the most picturesque of fishing towns. Batalha, a monastery erected to commemorate a Portuguese victory over the Castilians, blends Gothic and Manueline styles in typical and masterly fashion. Nearby Alcobaça, too, with its Cistercian monastery and church, founded c. 1152, is filled with history and holiness.

FATIMA

Ten miles east of Batalha you reach the shrine that has made Portugal particularly famous in America. Most Americans tend to think of Fatima as second only to Lourdes; the Portuguese have given it, of course, first place among shrines of Our Lady. I must confess that, having seen Lourdes first, I found Fatima a bit disappointing. For one thing, at Lourdes there is the constant flow of pilgrims, attending the infirm in a ceaseless mood of corporate love and prayer. Even when the faithful pray singly, they pray together. Fatima, on the other hand, unless you are fortunate enough to visit it on the thirteenth of the month (especially May and October), is a lonely place. Moreover, the surroundings are depressingly ugly, bleak, with none of the majesty of Lourdes. The colossal plaza, which the Portuguese say is twice as large as St. Peter's in Rome, seems featureless and barren. And little can be said in defense of the basilica.

Yet, I personally have nothing but gratitude to the people who invited me to visit the families of the children who saw Our Lady. And I am quite aware of the abundant good that Fatima has done to Portugal. Perhaps, after all, this is an authentic and superior form of religious pilgrimage: austere, unconsoling, severely penitential. In that case,

Fatima is ideal. These cautionary remarks are intended, not to discourage you from making the Fatima pilgrimage—rather the contrary—but to save you from feeling, as do so many who have gone there unwarned, somewhat let down when you go.

TOMAR

At Fatima you are not far from Tomar, which has a claim to being Portugal's finest town. This is where the Cortes accepted Philip II of Spain as king of Portugal, thus inaugurating what the Portuguese call their "Period of Spanish Captivity" (1580-1640). The Church of Christ, built in the twelfth century for the Knights Templars, is extraordinarily impressive, as are the cloister and chapter hall in their Manueline style.

COIMBRA

Coimbra, just to the north, must on no account be missed. It is the Oxford-Cambridge of Portugal, seat of one of the world's oldest universities (1290 is its date of foundation), numbering among its alumni Camoëns, St. Anthony and Premier Salazar, among many other illustrious men. The library is its most absorbing building. However, even apart from the university, Coimbra has a unique place in Portuguese annals. It was the nation's first capital, and in the Sé Velha ("Old

Cathedral") you will find tombs of the first two kings, Alfonso Henriques and Sanchez I.

The ancient church and convent of Santa Clara have a great history and offer a stunning view of the city. The church of Santa Cruz is the first professed church of the Society of Jesus, and that of São Tiago (Santiago would be the Spanish equivalent; St. James, the English) has a long spiritual heritage which you are quick to sense.

OPORTO

Some sixty miles north is Portugal's second city, capital of the Douro province, situated at the mouth of the Douro River—Oporto. The name is really two words: "O" meaning "the" and "porto" meaning "port." For Oporto is *the* port; the very name of Portugal is derived from it. An intensely vigorous and proud city, it has some of the attitude toward Lisbon that Barcelona feels toward Madrid—the city of work as opposed to the mere seat of government. Citizens of Oporto are called Portuenses, but are nicknamed "Tripeiros" ("tripe-eaters"), because (according to one of several explanations), when Don Henrique killed all the cattle of the area in 1415, civilians had nothing but tripe to eat. Lisboetas too have a nickname—"Alfacinhas"—but the derivation I have not been able to uncover. Oporto is, of course, the wine capital of Portugal, where port wine is made and shipped. Here vintage port may be bought for almost nothing.

THE NORTH

Still farther to the north is medieval Guimarães, where Portugal's first king was born; and Braga, once a capital, and still one of the most picturesque cities of the country. The shrine of Bom Jesus ("Good Jesus"), on Mount Espinho, is known for its devout pilgrims, to whom it affords a stupendous panorama, as well as inner graces. Finally, if you can spare the time and wish to see one of the greenest and most charming valleys anywhere in Europe, go north to the Minho. This river divides Portugal from that part of Spain (Galicia) which speaks almost the same language, where you will be able to investigate prehistoric Celtic villages, with their round stone houses atop hills. Here on this remote frontier between seldom-visited parts of two countries, a boat ride is a very special kind of experience, as I happily recall. It was my primitive form of entry into Portugal—by hired row boat in the early morning fog.

EVORA

Back in the south, you will find Evora a cross-section of Portugal's long history. Remarkably preserved colonnades of the temple of Diana will link you in imagination to the Roman past. City walls, the splendid Romanesque cathedral and vestiges of Moorish occupation will carry you along through the centuries. Here you will be reminded that, in all the world, few countries of comparable size can point pridefully to such a fecund and diverse tradition of cultures—one flowing into the other.

FRANCE

If the French are, of all peoples, the most given to generalizations, they themselves and their land defy nearly every generalization about them. Descartes' "clear and distinct idea" may be reckoned a French ideal, true, and though there are sunnier lands—Italy, for example, or Spain or Greece —in none are we more conscious of light itself. Not the relentless, piercing light of Naples or Granada, but a graduated, subtle light, as nuanced as a Pascal "Thought" or a line by Baudelaire.

Every tint, shade and value in the light that man sees by is to be found in France. You see it throughout French painting—from the wispy softness of Corot at one period, or his sharpness at another, to the stabbing yellows of Van Gogh (French by adoption, as many another painter) or the sculpturesque blues of Cézanne, through the luminous experience of the Impressionists, who explored light in all its dimensions.

Little wonder that, back in the twelfth and thirteenth centuries, it was in France that the full glory of stained glass—translucence itself—and of Gothic, the architecture of light, burst into dazzling being. Otto von Simson, who, in his *The Gothic Cathedral,* has written as knowledgeably as anyone on the Gothic period, shows that Abbot Suger, proponent of the style, was explicitly con-

cerned with creating a luminous architecture—
"matter transfigured by light." For light itself is
something more than earthly. It is "that power to
which our entire existence is mysteriously ordered." It is a symbol of God.

PARIS

It is hard not to start your pilgrimage of France
with Paris. At least if you arrive by plane, you
can scarcely avoid seeing Paris first. It is, of
course, the "Ville Lumière"—the "City of Light."
However, if you expect it to be full of the
garish sort of light you left in Times Square or
Piccadilly Circus, you deserve to be disappointed.
The light one looks for on a pilgrimage is not
principally connected with electricity, though the
French have certainly learned to use electricity to
advantage, playing beams of luminosity on their
cathedrals, their chateaux, their other monuments.
(One of the treats which you will surely not want
to miss is an evening of "Son et Lumière"—
"Sound and Light"—an ingenious French con-
fection, which we shall discuss when treating the
chateaux of the Loire valley.)

What you do first in Paris will depend on the
time of day you arrive. If it's early morning, why
not go straight to Notre-Dame, the city's heart,
for Mass? If it's midday and clear, you can do
worse than to go to the **Eiffel Tower,** like an honest tourist, and enjoy one of the world's supreme
visual delights. Artificial it is, of course. But the

view of Paris from each of the levels (stop and enjoy each of them) of the Tower is such that you would think that Paris had been built to be seen from the Tower. Actually the Tower was constructed in 1889 for the World's Fair and has several times narrowly escaped destruction as a monstrosity. Do, however, make sure that it is a clear day and that you have a map of the city at hand. The Tower is a far greater wonder than you suspect. Surely it is one of the most influential works in the history of architecture. After its construction, it was just a matter of time before the skyscraper would be conceived and executed.

When you come down (and provided the temperature is not too warm), walk along the Seine, taking the Quai d'Orsay side, toward **Notre-Dame.** Few walks in any city anywhere can match these miles of splendor, especially now that many monumental buildings have been cleaned. (For years they were allowed to accumulate a hideous patina of soot, but this misfortune has now been remedied in great part.)

I hope you approach Notre-Dame as the evening sun is setting it aglow. Then be sure to enter the cathedral, move up to the point where nave and transepts cross; look back at the west rose window and the two transept rose windows in all their glory. The other windows will probably disappoint you. They are not really ancient at all, but are rather deplorable replacements of the great medieval glass that once made Notre-Dame even more splendid than it is today. However, when

you realize something of the history of Paris and
the destruction wrought by irreligious vandals
(and religious ones too—often in the name of
"good taste"), you marvel that Notre-Dame stands
at all. Even bereft of much of its color and ornament, and despite the appalling emendations contributed by the centuries, Notre-Dame remains an
almost perfect Gothic structure, a tribute to Our
Lady, the Mother of God, and to the imagination
and skill of medieval artisans.

You will, of course, climb to the towers for a
totally different view of Paris—provided your
heart and energy allow the effort. And you will
want to stroll reverently around the apse, pausing
at the monument to the late Cardinal Suhard (one
of our century's greatest spiritual leaders) and
at the pillar where Paul Claudel was converted
(ask one of the sextons to point it out). When
you come back outside, allow plenty of time,
day or night, to stroll around Notre-Dame for a
leisurely view of every angle. Be especially sure
to find a place to sit contemplatively nearby.

More problems of choice will now confront you.
At least spare a few hours for a prayerful, exalting
visit to **La Sainte Chapelle** (the "Holy Chapel"),
just five minutes away from Notre-Dame. Hidden
away now in one of the courtyards of the Palais
de Justice, it is one of Paris' finest treasures. I recall an art teacher once telling me that entering the
Holy Chapel was like entering an amethyst. It is
an even more precious gem despite the ravages of
time and restorers. One thing will sadden you. The

Holy Chapel is a shrine without its precious relics. The relics of Our Lord's Passion, brought to Paris by St. Louis, called for a worthy house. The saint spared nothing to make it such. The upper chapel is almost purely a framework for stained glass, and while much of the glass that you see today is restored, the total effect is superb. Only in Chartres will you find a more overpowering ensemble of stained glass (though individual windows, such as those of Bourges are superior). Try to see the Holy Chapel at different hours and in different light.

You will find much to fascinate you as you walk along the Left Bank, with its chain of open-air bookstalls. Take time to visit **Saint-Séverin,** especially to participate in Mass there. For liturgists Saint-Séverin is a shrine of living worship. An ancient church (worth visiting in its own historic right), it is a center of liturgical experimentation in Paris, and, for that matter, the world. You will probably find the Mass there more moving, as you share in it, than in any other church.

You are not too far from the oldest church in Paris, Saint-Germain-des-Prés, a favorite of historians and architects. Much of the history of France can be seen and savored in a visit here. Just five minutes away is another world, centered around another church that has influenced religious life and sentiment in modern times— **Saint-Sulpice.** The influence, it need hardly be said, has not been altogether happy. In fact, "Saint-Sulpice art" is the term used for the sugary

type of work that the Germans call *Kitsch* and
New Yorkers call "Barclay Street," and which
some years ago (in an article in the *Catholic Art
Quarterly*) I suggested we call "Googawdery."
But, as so often happens, the original Saint-Sulpice
is somewhat less offensive than the many copies.
Try to hear the great organ, especially when
Marcel Dupré plays it.

Unprepossessing in terms of architectural interest, but one of the key spiritual shrines of the
world, is the Vincentian church popularly known
as **"Rue du Bac."** Here you enter the realm of
St. Vincent de Paul, undoubtedly one of Christendom's most lovable saints; of St. Louise de Maril-
lac; of the Miraculous Medal. Pilgrim and visiting
priests are particularly fond of celebrating Mass at
"Rue du Bac"—celebrated for its hospitality in a
city with little reputation for that virtue.

One of Paris' most distinguished eyesores must
also be visited. Like many another building that
one finds easy to criticize from photographs or at
a distance, **Sacré-Coeur,** the basilica of the Sacred
Heart in Montmartre, silences one in its presence.
Towering over Paris, the enormous Byzantine
sanctuary was built in reparation to Our Lord and
has become a true center of prayer and devotion.
Jesuits think of it as near the place where St.
Ignatius and his first followers pledged themselves
to Christ, August 15, 1534. There is a chapel
commemorating this event, but the exact location
is down the hill, in the chapel of Saint-Denis,
within an area now occupied by a convent. Also

on Montmartre, the ancient and interesting church of Saint-Pierre contains unusually fine modern stained glass.

Purely from the historical viewpoint, however, the church that I personally find most absorbing, but which is bypassed by most pilgrims, tourists and native Frenchmen, is technically not in Paris but in the rather unsightly suburb of Saint-Denis, to the north and east of the city. This is the **Abbey of Saint-Denis,** where kings of France were crowned and where most of them are buried. It is, historians agree, the mother church of Gothic. This was the church which Abbot Suger deliberately designed (the new choir, especially) to express light. Suger was no Puritan; he believed that man needs visual beauty to rise to the beauty of God.

The kings, from early Dagobert I (c. 639) throughout history, who were buried in the many picturesque sepulchres to be seen in Saint-Denis, were not allowed to lie untroubled. During the vicissitudes of the French Revolution, their bones were disinterred and unceremoniously flung about. Later they were gathered, helter-skelter, in the rear of the church, where they now lie in anonymous dignity, covered by a vast slab of black marble. Their names are carved, one after the other, on this slab, which, more than any monument I know, expresses the transience and tragedy of human grandeur.

Returning to Paris, you want to "do" a number of the obvious things that visitors "do." **The**

Louvre, for instance, is the largest art museum in the world and surely one of the best. There are literally miles of corridor to explore, but you will do well to plan your visits, allowing energy and time to see the principal treasures (not just the "Mona Lisa"). I suggest that you go to the Louvre in the morning, when you are fresh, and that you take a taxi, in order to allow all your physical energy for the actual visit. The approach suggested in *Holiday*'s volume "Paris" is excellent. In any case, be sure to see the "Winged Victory" and the "Venus de Milo" (though not the greatest Greek statuary extant, probably the most popular), the Salle de Sept Metres ("Seven-meter Room") the Grande Galerie and the Galerie de Medicis (which contains the indescribably lovely "Avignon Pietà"). For Impressionistic painting, it is the Musée du Jeu de Paume; for modern art, the Musée d'Art Moderne.

And, of course, you will want to visit that ironic monument, the imposing Arc de Triomphe. The view of the city from the top of the Arc, one of the most splendid anywhere, will almost make you forgive Napoleon. Nor will you neglect the Opéra, the Madeleine and the overpowering Place de la Concorde, severely classical and French. Just outside the capital, is Versailles, a standing symbol of Louis XIV, who did so much to make his country the capital of all Europe. And, nearby is the château of Fontainebleau. Francis I built the magnificent palace, chief glory of French Renaissance architecture.

LOURDES

As you leave Paris, you will wonder what to do next. If you are exhausted with grandeur and monuments, this may be the moment for a sound, spiritual rest. Nowhere can this retreat be better accomplished than in Lourdes, perhaps the most beloved shrine of all the West. Unless you have unlimited energy, the practical way to reach Lourdes is by plane—which will allow you more hours of repose than if you made the long trip by train or car.

Little needs to be said about Lourdes, since, of all familiar sanctuaries, it has become the most familiar through novels and film. You have probably already heard gruesome tales of the "horrid commercialism" that "spoils" Lourdes. Don't be dissuaded by that half-truth. True, the town has become principally a network of hotels and shops where every manner of religious bric-a-brac confronts the visitor. However, you are not there to see the town. Find a place to stay (most hotels are overpriced, but there's nothing you can do about that, except offer it up penitentially; you're on a pilgrimage, remember), make your purchases of rosaries or medals for friends back home, and leave the town with dispatch.

Once you cross the bridge onto the land of the grotto, you leave mundane vulgarity behind you. Somehow, despite the dismal architecture of the basilica (almost rivaling that of Lisieux and Paris'

Sacré-Coeur in sheer ugliness), the entire area gives you a sense of holiness. Voices are spontaneously hushed, save when raised in praise of God and God's Mother. Little musical distinction as the tune of the "Lourdes' Hymn" may possess, you will thrill to it as you join the thousands who sing it every evening during the candle light procession. You will also be glad you once memorized the chant Credo No. 3—not the finest of Gregorian chants, but the best known internationally, and, indeed, a sort of Catholic international anthem. The *unam, sanctam, catholicam et apostolicam Ecclesiam* phrases will stir you at Lourdes as probably nowhere else in the world.

There are, of course, other processions in which you will prayerfully participate. Lourdes is a social place, where our religion is shared by pilgrims of every nationality, where you will sense the Church's oneness amid diversity. But there is plenty of opportunity for personal (if not strictly "private") meditation and prayer. The presence of others, paradoxically, does not interfere; rather, the fact that everyone is praying and helping others will make it easier for you to commune with God. Allow yourself several days at Lourdes and you will be refreshed and ready to enjoy the other sublime delights of France.

CATHEDRALS, CASTLES AND SHRINES

Chief among these are, of course, the cathedrals. For France is, pre-eminently, the Land of Cathedrals. You will face an *embarras de richesse,* and your selection will have to be made somewhat ruthlessly. Let me suggest an order of greatness, then leave it to you to decide how many you have time and strength to visit.

Since you have already seen Notre-Dame de Paris, there is now no problem about your first choice. Any historian or artist would tell you that it must be **Chartres.** Fortunately, the cathedral is near Paris and easily accessible. Why not start out early in the morning, by car, bus, or train, and begin your day at Chartres participating in the Holy Sacrifice? As you approach the town, continue scanning the horizon for the great towers that rise from the plains of Beauce. Few sights blend nature and man's creation so movingly as does the vision of Chartres rising out of the wheat fields. Generations of pilgrims have tingled to this before you. For even long before the present cathedral was built, this was a holy place, one of Mary's earliest shrines.

Chartres deserves preparatory study. If you have time to read only one book before going to France, you can hardly do better than to choose Henry Adams' classic *Mont-Saint-Michel and Chartres* (get the paperback and read it on board ship). Though not a Catholic, Adams does show a deep feeling for the devotion to God's Mother that inspired the creation of Chartres and many other medieval sanctuaries. For a more strictly analytical view, you will also enjoy reading through Hans Jantzen's authoritative work, *High*

Gothic, or if you want more illustrations and can afford to own them, Hürlimann's and Bony's *French Cathedrals.*

Adams and other students of Chartres have quoted documents that tell us of the actual building of the cathedral. Robert de Mont-Saint-Michel records, in 1144, that one could see "the faithful harnessed to carts, laden with stones, timbers, corn and whatever might be needed for the work of building . . . And this, not only here, but almost everywhere in France . . . Men and women dragging heavy loads, praising in song the miracle which God was performing before their eyes." And, at the same time, Abbot Haimon describes the scene, where "lords and princes, full of riches and honors, even women of noble birth" carried gifts for the cathedral; meanwhile, "though more than a thousand people are there, deep silence reigns, no word is heard, not even a whisper."

But, as Etienne Gilson sagaciously observed, "piety does not dispense with technique," and no cathedral, least of all Chartres, could have been conceived or erected by some vague collective devotion. There has been a romantic exaggeration about the anonymity of medieval art, as though we knew no names of architects or craftsmen. However, in the case of Chartres, the legend is true. The master architect here is known simply as the "Master of Chartres."

Approaching the town through the wheat fields of Beauce, you sense what pilgrims for a thousand years have sensed. The towers, as in a vision,

point prayerfully upward. Soon you see that they
are from different epochs—the left one (technically called the "North Tower") is a late flamboyant creation of extraordinary delicacy, and the
other an early marvel of pure Romanesque. We
are fortunate that both were left standing, para-
gons of their separate styles.

No one has defined the mystery of Chartres'
unique glory. The strictly architectural proportions
of the interior are surely crucial; but even more so
is the unearthly light that floats through the cathedral, ever shifting as the sun follows its course.
For this reason, try to see Chartres at every moment of the day (I have walked around it many
times even at night). Of the 186 stained glass windows, 152 were created at the peak of their art,
each an individual masterpiece. You will have
your own favorites; mine are the Jesse Window,
right of center over the main entrance, and "Our
Lady of the Beautiful Glass," near the altar on
the epistle side. The one is cool and classic and
heavenly; the other warm, romantic, incarnate.

Rivaling its own stained glass, is Chartres'
statuary. Some 1800 carved figures remain in an
astonishing state of preservation, having escaped
the holy wrath of iconoclasts and the savagery of
the Revolution. Compared to such splendor,
Notre-Dame de Paris seems destitute indeed and
ravished. The entire vision of divine revelation is
here presented in images that can be grasped. We
find all the world Christ-centered, the Royal Por-
tico showing Christ in his glory, surrounded by

the four evangelists, the prophets, and the liberal arts.

To make even a cursory study of all the statues of Chartres would take many days. The practical thing might be to concentrate on just a few, with a general grasp of the architectural function of the assembly. For Chartres—somewhat like the Parthenon—links its statuary with the whole structure, a symbol of the visible Church and pledge of the heavenly Jerusalem. No wonder that an old catechism, describing what one should do on entering a cathedral, advised: "Take holy water, bless yourself, genuflect, and then go around to see the windows and statues." For these, even after the invention of printing, remain visible Bibles, unfolding the divine Word in images and symbols that still move the heart.

Near Paris, within the ancient Isle de France, are many other great Gothic cathedrals, the chief being Amiens and Rheims. Both are a bit later and more soaring than Chartres. **Amiens,** considered by Viollet-le-Duc (the great nineteenth-century authority on Gothic) "*the* Gothic church par excellence," seems even more transparently built than Chartres, with a verticality that is hard to match, save at Beauvais. But Beauvais was never completed, even though the choir and transepts are among the most impressive monuments to the Gothic spirit.

Rheims has been called the Queen of French Cathedrals. In some ways it is more graceful, surely more ornamental than its rivals. Quite appropriately, it was used for the crowning of France's royalty. If you happen to be traveling by car, by all means stop between Amiens and Rheims and enjoy the Cathedral of Laon, with its many towers high above the plains, crowning an impressive hill town. And you will surely be more astute than the Frenchman I talked to in Laon. I mentioned that I was eager to see Rheims cathedral. "Yes," he agreed, "they say it's beautiful." He had lived his whole life only thirty miles away, but had never bothered to see it for himself.

We do know the names of the chief architects who designed Amiens and Rheims—Robert de Luzarches and Jean d'Orbais, respectively. These great creators knew the work of their predecessors and contemporaries, and while preserving their own originality, incorporated others' discoveries. Jantzen, in his *High Gothic*, compares the façades of these and other cathedrals, showing how Jean d'Orbais learned from both Paris and Laon, yet managed to create something totally original in Rheims.

Among the cathedrals which I am most reluctant to omit—but which I hope you have time to visit—are Bourges (with its five porticoes and astonishing stained glass); Le Mans (with possibly the most impressive of cathedral choirs); Sens (in early Gothic, possibly a model for Chartres, Amiens, and Rheims); Rouen (representing all styles of Gothic, from the simplest to the highly ornate Tower of Butter).

While in Rouen, by the way, be sure not to miss

several churches which rival the cathedral—Saint-Ouen and Saint-Maclou. It is just as well, at this point, to remember that not all of the great churches of French Gothic are cathedrals. There are literally hundreds of other buildings of great architectural quality, built during the high creative period of the cathedrals.

Nor should we entirely identify Gothic with French. Although it is true, by and large, the closer one comes to Paris the purer the Gothic, there is a wondrous school of Gothic in Britain, and (somewhat less, but still important) there is the Gothic of Germany and Spain, even of Italy. Equally noteworthy is the fact that Romanesque is a living style in France. Now is the time to turn our attention to a few treasures of French Romanesque.

In eastern France, midway between Bourges and Sens, looms one of medieval France's high holy places. We are now in the heart of Burgundy, not far from Dijon (with its fine cathedral of Saint-Bénigne and Burgundian church of Notre-Dame) and Beaune with its Hospice. Not as spectacular as Mont-Saint-Michel, since it is surrounded by land, not water, **Vézelay** is another place of spiritual and cultural pilgrimage. High above the valley at Vézelay is the shrine of St. Mary Magdalene, rich in sculpture, the very spot where St. Bernard preached his crusade. Although the sculpture has been marred by iconoclasts, the ensemble remains magnificent.

For a group of Romanesque statuary that can

hardly be matched, however, continue toward the
south, halfway to Paray-le-Monial, to **Autun.** In
the past few years, Gislebertus has become a
household name in the field of sculpture, for
modern scholarship has identified him as the artist
who created virtually all the statutes in the church
of Saint-Lazare in Autun. He seems to have
worked between 1125 and 1135, and to have enjoyed fame in his lifetime; however, only in 1961,
with Trianon Press' publication of Denis Grivot's
and George Zarnecki's careful study of his Autun
sculpture, has Gislebertus become, deservedly, if
belatedly, a world figure.

(A concentrated area of time and space—less
than the hundred years from the mid-eleventh to
the mid-twelfth century; and on an axis of less
than 150 miles, roughly from Dijon to Grenoble
—made France the heartland of religious life.
Then and there, four of history's greatest monasteries had their beginnings or reached their
peaks of influence: Cluny, Cîteaux, Clairvaux and
La Grande Chartreuse. Although not great centers
of pilgrimage today, they are of exceptional interest to anyone aware of the Church's long and
diverse spiritual heritage.)

It will prove hard to know where to turn after
Autun—southward toward **Paray-le-Monial** or
westward. Paray is, of course, celebrated for the
apparitions of Our Lord to St. Margaret Mary, in
the seventeenth century. Since then the devotion
to the Sacred Heart has become a large part of
Catholic life.

Apart from the fine Romanesque abbey church, however, little at Paray appeals to the eye, and the pilgrimage, say, to the recent basilica of Blessed Claude La Colombière in this holy spot tends to be an austere rather than a delightful experience.

Not too far away, you may stop briefly at Nevers, an otherwise undistinguished city, to venerate St. Bernadette Soubirous' body, which lies incorrupt in a glass reliquary. And there, in the same chapel, is interred the heart of Father Thomas F. Price, one of the founders of Maryknoll.

Of exquisite proportions, indeed one of the rarest examples of French Romanesque, is the abbey church of Saint-Benoît-sur-Loire. You will profit by attending the divine office and venerating the relics of St. Benedict. And just a few miles away, in one of the oldest and most moving of small French churches, Germigny-des-Prés, you will discover ancient Byzantine mosaics.

If it were not a bit difficult to reach, **Mont-Saint-Michel** in northwestern France would be too obvious a choice to need recommendation. Students of art and travel guides rightly rhapsodize over what is called "the marvel of the West," "a miracle of conception and design," and the like. You will not be disappointed, whether you approach the Mount through mist, as it rises from the sea, or on a bright summer day. The abbey embodies a number of styles, from early Romanesque through all the phases of Gothic, and, despite the centuries that have gone into its making, it does achieve a mysterious harmony within itself—a magic blend of man's work with God's creation. Unhappily, it is a secularized museum at present, and your guide may scowl at you, as ours did, if you venture to chant a "Salve Regina" before the deserted high altar.

Towering Mont-Saint-Michel is appropriately dedicated to St. Michael, since it *does* seem the right thing to meet the archangel halfway. Another shrine dedicated to St. Michael—at **Le Puy** in central France—even if no rival, is very rewarding to the pilgrim. Here, atop a volcanic rock rising wondrously from the valley, St. Michael is also venerated. In fact, the entire town of Le Puy is well worth a visit. During the Middle Ages it too was a pilgrimage center. Its cathedral is a sturdy example of Romanesque, with a flavor of Byzantine, suggesting that the town was once a great center of international travel. For the pilgrim routes, as Dawson has reminded us, served also as the routes of commerce and culture.

Mont-Saint-Michel links Normandy and Brittany, and though there may be comparatively less of architectural interest in Brittany than in other regions of France, the province can claim a special type of person and Christian. At times, as you travel through France, you will be disappointed at the Sunday practice of the Faith; in Brittany one could imagine oneself in Ireland. In fact, the ancient languages of Brittany and Ireland are distantly related, as are the peoples themselves.

Normandy, too, is of great interest, even apart

from Rouen, its principal city. The cathedrals of
Coutances and Bayeux are splendid, while the city
of Caen, with its two Romanesque abbeys, marks
an important chapter in the history of religious
architecture. But, save for some of its older buildings, such as the cathedral, Lisieux and its monuments to the Little Flower can best be visited from
afar in prayer. St. Therese deserved better.

Moving down into western France, we meet
Angers, with its distinguished cathedral and massive, seventeen-tower castle. Still more remarkable
is the incredible collection of Flemish tapestries
contained in the castle. Dating from the late Middle Ages, these tapestries include a set that treats
the Apocalypse, which for sheer splendor matches
the most thrilling mosaics or paintings or glass
anywhere.

From Angers it is only a short drive to Solesmes
Abbey, where Solemn Mass or Vespers will provide you with an unforgettable spiritual and es-
thetic experience. Nowhere is the refinement, subtlety and spirituality of Gregorian chant more
evident than in this great sanctuary of prayer and
scholarship.

You are now very near **Tours,** capital city of
the Loire valley, and famed for its ornate cathedral
and shrine of St. Martin, one of the most influential saints during the period of the making of
Europe. The Loire valley is best known, however, more for secular than sacred tours. It is here
that the nobility of France and many of the royalty
built their châteaux. Each of these is a unique

structure, and it is hard to pick a favorite. Chambord is largest, with its 440 rooms and many towers. Chenonceau, built over the Cher river, is in some ways the most graceful. But there are dozens to choose from. And, if you can afford an evening, you will enjoy the dramatic spectacles called "Son et Lumière," where with sound and light the entire history of the individual château is excitingly retold. The presentations, done here with considerable imagination and taste, have been less successfully copied elsewhere.

Between Tours and Poitiers was fought a battle that historians consider one of the most decisive in history. It was there, in 732, that Charles Martel, Major Domo of the Frankish kings, turned back the apparently superior army of Moslems and saved Christendom. Where exactly this historic battle was fought is not pointed out. But the area is exciting for anyone who thinks in terms of the meaning of history.

THE SOUTH

Poitiers, Angoulême, Périgueux and Bordeaux, as one moves southward, are all impressive in their cathedrals and other churches. To the east of Bordeaux, however, is one of the most important of prehistoric centers of culture, the Dordogne Valley. In the last few years, caves at **Lascaux,** Les Eyzies, Font-de-Gaume and others have become known throughout the world. Off the beaten track, they are nevertheless worth

every bit of the trouble required to visit them. One
caution, however: since a restricted number of
visitors is allowed into Lascaux every day, be sure
to arrive early enough to be included. If you are
so fortunate, you will witness a sight lost to man
for eons, that will enable you to bridge spiritually
the tens of thousands of years separating us from
our paleolithic ancestors. Much like Altamira,
in Spain, this area offers a particular human
experience unmatched elsewhere.

As you move eastward toward Provence, you
will surely visit Albi with its brooding cathedral-
fortress, a unique structure. To the south lies
Carcassonne, the fortified town that more than
any other suggests the middle ages. You may feel
that there is something too good to be true about
Carcassonne, and you will be right. Much of it has
been reconstructed during the past century, and
the result is just a bit too stagey to be quite satisfying. A good place to take pictures, though.

Provence, from its name, an ancient Roman
province, is today the most Roman (almost
Italian) part of France. Here you encounter another light, that of the Mediterranean, the light
so appealing to painters Van Gogh and Cézanne.
Here too is an endless variety of architecture—
from the Greek, the Roman, the European, to the
very modern buildings of Le Corbusier and the
lovely Matisse chapel at Vence.

You will surely visit **Nîmes,** with its Maison
Carrée (the "Square House" beloved of Thomas
Jefferson, who was inspired by it to bring the
Roman style to our country) and the unbelievable

Roman bridge and arena. You may be fortunate enough to witness a bullfight or some spectacle in the arena here or at Arles. **Arles** was once a great capital of the entire region, and with its superb church of Saint-Trophime, its Roman theater and Roman arena, among other wonders, will make you want to spend some time in leisurely contemplation.

To the north, just an hour away, is **Avignon.** There the Popes lived from 1308-1377, in a palace which is severe but most imposing. The stone of Avignon is particularly attractive and golden when seen in the setting sun—another gift of France's uncanny light. Aix-en-Provence rivals Arles in antiquity and interest. Of course, if you want to see a large, lively French city, Marseilles is there for you. And for rest and entertainment, there is the Riviera.

OTHER REGIONS

Each section of France has its special charm, its vintage, its shrines, its art. Choice becomes very difficult, indeed, almost arbitrary, especially when one reflects on the many areas not covered here. The eastern part, nudging the Rhine, has a beauty of its own, with stately cities like Strasbourg and Metz, boasting of cathedrals that match almost any in the world apart from the "Big Four" (Paris, Chartres, Amiens, Rheims). In quest of relics of Joan of Arc, you will perhaps stop at Domrémy. If your taste runs more toward painting, you will surely stop in Colmar to view Gruenewald's masterpiece, the "Altarpiece of Isenheim," a polyptych including the piercing "Crucifixion," one of the most intense works in all art. And there are many other shrines to be visited, such as Ars (with its memories of St. John Vianney), Notre-Dame de La Salette in the French Alps, Notre-Dame de la Garde in Marseilles (an architectural horror, despite its sacred tradition), and a number of holy places in Brittany, where the *calvaires* and *pardons* are an experience quite unlike any other in my memory.

Two cities in the Rhone valley are particularly venerable in Church history: **Lyons** and **Vienne.** Both are thought of as mother churches of France. St. Pothinus, St. Irenaeus and other very early saints are remembered in Lyons, and both cities are celebrated for Ecumenical Councils (the thirteenth and fourteenth, 1245 and 1274, in Lyons; the fifteenth in Vienne, 1311-1312). A great city, Lyons possesses little charm, except for the shrine of Notre-Dame de Fourvière (which is not physically attractive) and the cathedral.

If, as Paul Valéry once said, the happy combination of fantasy and logic is a specific characteristic of the European spirit, no country can be called more entirely European than France. With its culture of balance, measure, proportion, clarity, subtlety—where Latin, Celt and Teuton meet in a dynamic synthesis that is never quite completed —France, Eldest Daughter of the Church, stands for Europe and the West. You can hardly fail to recognize in Paris your second capital, your own city of light.

BELGIUM

If you fly into Belgium, be sure to take a seat by the window, and try to choose a clear day. The view then will be an incredible mosaic of tiny, variegated farms, with at least a dozen villages, clustered picturesquely about the parish church, all within sight at one time. Smokestacks in abundance betoken the many industrial towns and cities. You soon realize that you are flying over one of the most densely populated areas in Europe, a land of thrift and energy and long civilization.

BRUSSELS AND GHENT

Brussels is not especially ancient, however, as European capitals go. True, the city has been there for a long time; both the great church of Sainte-Gudule and the Grand'Place will remind you of that. But Belgium has existed as an independent country only since 1830, and Brussels was not exceptionally important before that time. Thus, most of the capital is no more ancient than Washington, D.C., and it is a good deal less impressive, Americans find, than most older European large cities.

The Exposition ("l'Expo," they liked to call it) of 1958 was indeed an enormous success. Brussels took that occasion to do a certain amount of house

113

cleaning and painting. Consequently, the Grand'-Place, always an immense and imposing square, is now one of the handsomest in Europe. You will spend time well if you relax and enjoy it at leisure. The flamboyant Flemish blend of Gothic and baroque is unusually satisfying. Sainte-Gudule, the principal church, is hardly comparable to the great cathedrals of France or England, but you will enjoy a brief visit.

Brussels' fine Royal Gallery has a valuable collection of most of the artists you expect to see, except, surprisingly, Van Eyck, Belgium's great painter. ("Painters," it should be, for there were two Van Eyck brothers, who constantly collaborated.) The masterpiece of the Van Eycks, however, is just a few miles away, in the cathedral of Saint-Bavon, Ghent. This is "The Adoration of the Sacred Lamb," one of the supreme works in all the art of painting. It is as fresh and exhilarating as the day it was finished.

Ghent is in other ways a fascinating city, with its quays, guild houses, castles, old abbeys and delightful Flemish domestic architecture. In its Museum of Fine Arts you will find splendid Flemish tapestries and paintings, among them Hieronymus Bosch's great "Carrying of the Cross."

BRUGES

Bruges (a rival of Amsterdam for the title of "Venice of the North") is a living museum. Fortunately the area you will want to see is small, hardly half a square mile, and can be comfortably encompassed on foot. You will be sure to visit at least the following: the Grand'Place, with the Governor's Palace and the immense 270-foot belfry, whose carillon is played several times a week; the Chapel of the Holy Blood; the Town Hall; the Groeninge Museum (with several of the finest works of Memling, and of Van Eyck, particularly his monumental "Virgin with Canon van der Paele," of Bosch and Gerard David); the Hans Memling Museum in St. John's Hospital, another superlative collection of that master; the Béguinage; the church of Notre-Dame, in which you will see Michelangelo's "Virgin and Child," one of his few paintings to be found outside Italy.

ANTWERP

Antwerp has taken Bruges' place as the great port of the area; in fact, it now claims to be the third port of the world. Regrettably, a band of fanatical puritans destroyed most of the sacred art of Antwerp and the surrounding region on August 18, 1566, in what has been described as a "St. Bartholomew Massacre of Sacred Art." Thus, most of Antwerp's artistic treasures are post-Reformation.

The cathedral, with its six columned aisles and immense transepts, is the fourth largest in Europe. Its fame, however, rests largely on three of Rubens' major works: his "Assumption of Our Lady" over the high altar, and the two companion master-

pieces, the "Elevation of the Cross" and the
"Descent from the Cross." Although Rubens was
born in Westphalia, he moved to Antwerp at the
age of ten and is claimed as Antwerp's most illustrious citizen. He is magnificently represented
in the local museum of fine arts, where there are
also superior works of Van Eyck and Van der
Weyden, as well as of Rubens' gifted disciples, Van
Dyck and Jordaens. Other important Rubens work
will be found in the churches of St. Augustine, St.
James and St. Paul. The painter and his family, including his two wives (two in succession, not
simultaneously), are buried in St. James' church.

MALINES

Malines (which the Flemish, who live there,
call Mechelen) is the religious capital, where the
cardinal-primate lives. (Brussels, in fact, is in
the diocese of Malines.) This picturesque city's
cathedral contains one of Van Dyck's masterpieces, an altarpiece of the Crucifixion. Nearby,
in St. John's church, you see yet another work of
the prolific Rubens, an altarpiece. In the church
of Notre-Dame is his famous "Miraculous Draught
of Fishes." The bells of the cathedral are known
all over the world, as is the splendid organ playing of Flor Peeters. He and his contemporary composers remind us that Belgium and Holland—the
Low Countries, as they were called—produced
leading composers of the Renaissance and of all

time; among them are Ockeghem, Obrecht, Josquin des Prés, and Lassus.

LOUVAIN

Louvain (called Leuven in Flemish) is known the world over as one of the great university towns. Though the victim of fearful havoc in both World Wars, it has twice risen again, a symbol of the indestructible Christian-Humanist spirit. The Hôtel de Ville is one of the finest examples of northern architecture, and there are several churches in a number of styles that are worth visiting. Indeed, some of the richest baroque in Europe can be found here, and the Béguinage church is not to be missed. Opposite the Hôtel de Ville, the late Gothic church of Saint-Pierre is a curiosity that must be seen to be believed—its pulpit represents the extreme of late baroque ornamentation. On the other hand, the simple shrine of St. John Berchmans, in the Jesuit church on Rue des Recollets, is devotional and suitable to the unpretentious young Belgian saint. On the altar you may venerate the saint's still incorrupt heart. His body is buried in the church of St. Ignatius, Rome.

GHEEL

Less than an hour's ride east of Antwerp, is Gheel, one of the most interesting, yet least publicized towns in Belgium. True, it now possesses an atomic reactor, but for eleven centuries Gheel has been one of the most humane and charitable towns in the world. For all this time, the inhabitants of Gheel have provided foster homes for the mentally ill. Although today there is a psychiatric hospital where modern methods are applied, the fundamental and most important aid to the ill continues: they are treated as human beings and live freely in homes of normal people. This difficult form of charity was started under religious auspices in connection with St. Dympna, an Irish saint said to have been beheaded here in the year 600. One of the least popular of saints, St. Dympna could surely be better known today, when we are so preoccupied with the problem of mental health. The approach to psychic illness associated with her name deserves wider study and imitation.

THE WALLOON COUNTRY

The Walloon (south and southeast) part of Belgium, where French is spoken rather than Flemish, is less celebrated for fine arts than the sections already mentioned. By and large, however, it is more attractive than the others in its natural scenery and special kind of charm. Yet Tournai, near the French border, is famed for its cathedral, which may be the finest in the country, a fine Hôtel de Ville, and several churches and public buildings of importance. There are also many castles in the Tournai vicinity. More castles

—châteaux—are found in the Meuse valley. You will be reminded of the Loire when you visit Freyr and Walzin. A good deal of archeological interest is attached to the many grottos near Han and Dinant, while Liége, the old city of prince-bishops, boasts a superb set of churches and museums.

Belgium, you will find, is as concentrated in treasures of humanity as it is in humanity itself.

HOLLAND

Holland (we really should say "The Netherlands," since Holland is properly only one province in the country; but popular mistakes have a way of sticking) is not a hard country for Americans to like and to feel at home in. The correlative problem is, rather, that it is a comparatively hard country for us to get excited about. Everything appears neat and civilized and charming and ever-so-bourgeois. Even the great churches, stripped by Reformers, have lost most of their color and seem barnlike.

Yet, if not precisely exciting, Holland is an eminently delightful land, with much more variety than the quick glance reveals. I even saw lovely blond children, bedecked in Indian feathers and garb, playing cowboys and Indians on the sedate streets of Amsterdam. Nor are the cities really alike, no two of them. In fact, the very language, mysterious as it is for us even if we know German, changes so much from region to region that Hollanders themselves, born only twenty miles apart, often find each other hard to understand.

AMSTERDAM

Amsterdam, the metropolis even if not the "capital," will repay a good, leisurely visit. Another "Venice of the North," it has substantial charm, even if it is not as romantic as Bruges or its namesake.

You will enjoy a boat trip through these canals, preferably toward evening. The Dutch, you will find, though not as fond of color as Mediterranean folk, do use it generously and judiciously, painting their windmills and boats with pleasant hues. Their houses tend to be built of picturesque black or brown bricks, with a good deal of white mortar etched in between, and with much white ornamentation in the windows. And with all the charm and the fifty canals crossed by five hundred bridges dividing the city into seventy islands, you never forget that this is a lively, not a museum city clutching desperately to what has been. Amsterdam is anything but that; it is very much of the present, modern, metropolitan with a rapidly growing population.

True, the museums are there, several of the finest in Europe. Indeed, any list of the top collections of painting in the world would surely include the Rijksmuseum ("National Museum"). It is situated in a pleasant spot near Amsterdam's two other great cultural shrines: the Concertgebouw ("Concert Building"), whose orchestra, one of the world's finest, has made Holland internationally celebrated as a musical country; and the Stedelijk Museum ("Municipal Museum"), containing more than a hundred works of Van Gogh, as well as a great deal of other, more modern art, some by the leading Dutch painters, Mondrian and others. Indeed, to find more Van Gogh in one place, you will have to visit the Kröller-Müller Museum in Otterlo, also in Holland.

The *pièce de résistance* of the Rijksmuseum is the most famous painting of Holland's most famous painter, Rembrandt's "Night Watch." It is beautifully mounted, perhaps more beautifully than any other painting in the world, in a spacious room where one may see it from almost any distance and angle. Within the room one may make an interesting study in composition too. For there are displayed copies of the painting before it was cut to fit the wall of the building where it was once kept; the differences between the work as Rembrandt conceived it—more open, not so crowded as it now seems, and with a slightly different centering—and the present shape make a fascinating study. It is remarkable that whoever did the cutting, managed to leave a masterpiece not far inferior to the original. Several cleanings, too, have changed the mood of the painting, and the museum now no longer calls it "Night Watch," but "The Company of Frans Banning Cocq," since the sources of light show that it was never a night scene at all. Rembrandt's great "Syndics," too, and his "Jewish Bride" are special treasures of the museum, as are four of Vermeer's loveliest paintings. There is a certain quality of modesty, serenity, civilized depth to the greatest of Dutch paintings, which have great appeal to us and seem to fit with what we already know of this courageous and industrious people. *Luctor et emergo* ("I struggle and rise up") is the appropriate motto of a nation that has literally built up its land from the sea.

Luctor et emergo has more than a geophysical meaning in Holland. The epic of its history, the struggle for independence, its immense commercial empire and rivalry with such powers as Spain and England (reflected in the unkind English epithets "Dutch uncle," "Dutch treat" and others), its fantastic influence all out of proportion to its size, has been written by Holland's great national poet, Vondel. Interestingly, Vondel was a Catholic convert in a country then overwhelmingly Protestant. Thus *Luctor et emergo* may also serve as the motto of Catholicism in Holland—the gradual growth from bare survival under centuries of discrimination and decades of severe persecution, to equality. You will find relatively few Catholic shrines in Holland, but those that are there have a rich meaning. In Amsterdam, of more than twenty monasteries that existed before the Reformation, only the Begijnhof (Béguinage) survived as a center, almost a bastion, of Catholicism during hard days. Today it is an interesting site to visit. At No. 35 Begijnhof, there is the Catholic Orientation Center for Foreigners which provides what its name suggests, guides and general information for any who wish to make use of its services. Among Catholic churches in Amsterdam, of which today there are many, St. Nicholas is the most prominent, though the seven-towered church of St. Willibrord is the largest in the country. Of the vestiges of the days of persecution, one of the most touching is at

No. 90 Oude Zijds Voorburgwal, where Mass was celebrated in hiding; the chapel is called, picturesquely, "Our Dear Lord in the Attic." It is near the Royal Palace.

Among other interesting sights in Amsterdam are the Rembrandt House (in the old Jewish section, which some believe helped stimulate the master's interest in Old Testament and Jewish subjects); the house where Anne Frank and her family hid from the Nazis (Prinsengracht 263); the very modern Opstanding Church; the new Children's Home in the western part of the city, and several nearby places such as Volendam, Aalsmeer, the island of Marken, and the town of Haarlem, home of the painter Frans Hals.

THE HAGUE

Holland's second city, often called the capital since the Parliament and many other government buildings are there, is The Hague. Thanks to its International Court of Justice, the Hague is also some sort of world capital. It is an elegant city, with handsome avenues and buildings. Most arresting for the visitor is the Mauritshuis, Holland's second museum. Occupying only a residence, it is intimate (somewhat like New York's Frick Museum) rather than exhaustingly large. Here again, appropriately, Rembrandt and Vermeer are dominant. "The Anatomy Lesson" and four magnificent self-portraits, together with the "Presentation in the Temple" give us some of the greatest of Rembrandt; while Vermeer's "View of Delft" will make you want to pay a visit to nearby Delft (do so). The "Girl with a Turban" is surely another of Vermeer's masterpieces. Among fifteen other museums in the Hague, the Gemeente offers a pleasant contrast, with its stress on Mondrian and other modern painters.

OTHER CITIES

Rotterdam is called the "Phoenix City," having risen wondrously from its ashes following the horrible destruction of World War II. This destruction, however, has made Rotterdam almost synonymous with modern architecture. The central Lijnbaan is a fascinating piece of redevelopment, planned by architects Van den Broek and Bakema. Marcel Breuer (who later did St. Johns' Abbey, Minnesota) designed the very interesting Bijenkorf Department Store, in front of which stands Naum Gabo's extravagant abstraction. It may be that too much had to be built too quickly, but much of Rotterdam, while impressive, I found unimaginative and repetitious.

You should also visit the Boymans–van Beuningen Museum, not as great as the Rijksmuseum or Mauritshuis, but splendidly representative of the great Dutch masters and others. Bosch's stirring "Prodigal Son," alone, would make this visit a delight.

Bosch's birthplace, almost fifty miles southeast of Rotterdam, is called Bois-le-Duc or 's Hertogen-

bosch, and is famous for its splendid cathedral
(with an eleventh-century tower, a thirteenth-cen-
tury chapel, and astonishing carvings). **Utrecht,**
where the renowned Cardinal Frings lives, is one
of the most ancient towns in Holland. Founded
by Dagobert I in the early seventh century (it
had St. Willibrord as its first bishop in 695),
at various times it has exerted a powerful influence
on the country. The cathedral tower is lofty and
imposing and offers a view of a large part of Holland. The university and several museums all show
the depth of tradition here.

Nijmegen, a city of seven hills, has a long history; it was a free city in the Holy Roman Empire and a residence of the Carolingian emperors.
The curfew and the city's finest square are both
named after "Keiser Karel" ("Emperor Charles—
the Great), and there are remains of his palace.
Nijmegen is a strong center of Catholicism, and,
appropriately, the birthplace of St. Peter Canisius
(1521-97), Doctor of the Church and the second
apostle of the Germanies. Nearby is the now-fa-
mous Holy Land Foundation, which reconstructs
the topography and, as much as possible, the mood
of the Holy Land.

Maastricht is actually an old Roman ford over
the Meuse (Trajectum ad Mosam having been
corrupted into "Maastricht"). In 382 St. Servatius
transferred his see there from Tongres. The church
named after him is, in fact, the oldest church in
the Netherlands, though it has been added to or
altered at various times. The crypt, containing the

tomb of St. Servatius, together with a key probably presented to him by Pope St. Damasus (376),
was rediscovered only in 1881. The bishop's feast
is celebrated with great enthusiasm on May 13.
Every seven years the entire month of July is
given over to festivals in his honor.

The Church in the Netherlands has grown so
vigorously that references that you sometimes hear
about "living in the Diaspora" now seem humor-
ous, for nowhere is religious life more alive and in
touch with the best of the contemporary world.
Much like neighboring Belgium and in some ways
like Ireland (where the Church was so long underprivileged), Holland has shown its spiritual vitality by becoming one of the world leaders in missionary activity. In proportion, no country has
shown itself more generous.

GREAT BRITAIN

On most Americans going to Europe no country will exert a firmer tug than Great Britain. Most of us are not English in any genetic sense—being without so much as a drop of English blood—yet, more often than not, language runs thicker than blood. Language is a vehicle of political thought and mood, national history and legend, indeed of just about everything that forms one's mentality or culture. The bonds are even closer when the language channels a matchless literature.

Even Americans of Irish descent, though understandably ambivalent in their feelings about England, hold intimate ties with the language and all that language carries. Long before their advent in America, the Irish came to speak the language of England. And so, whether or not your ancestry is British, and however much disaffection for Cromwell may linger in your family tradition, you, the American going to England, are in some way, going home.

LONDON

Such a homecoming presents problems, plainly, and especially if it is the first. For home may well have been glamorized beyond recognizable reality, and stark facts may disenchant. London, where you will probably start your tour (since all roads on land, sea and by air lead to and from London), offers little to impress the superficial viewer. Its buildings do not soar like New York's; its avenues are a poor second to those of Paris; it enjoys none of the gay color of Madrid, much less any of Rome's depth of antiquity and sacredness. Rather, it gives the impression of a vast, sprawling town (London Town, they used to call it), rambling off haphazardly in every direction, endlessly.

Fortunately, if you are to spend only a few days in London you can find most of the historic treasures within easy striking distance. If you want to move fast, avoiding the traffic bedlam, use the "Tube" (subway), which is expeditious and inexpensive. However, for short distances taxis are relatively cheap. Best of all, as always, do a lot of walking.

Westminster Abbey ("the Abbey") is neither technically in London nor is it a cathedral; yet, in many ways, it is the heart both of London and of England. The original London ("the City") is a small area, centered around St. Paul's and the financial district. But it is the Abbey where Britain's monarchs are crowned and where almost all of them from Edward the Confessor to George III are buried. You will not be able to see a coronation, of course, but you will see hundreds of tombs of saints and sinners, often side by side. Indeed, the Abbey is likely to depress you, as you find grave monuments to the Unknown Warrior,

as well as to well-known literary figures like
Chaucer, Spenser, Tennyson, Browning, Dickens,
Kipling and others. Much as we appreciate these
worthy folk, we find it hard to imagine them
buried in holy ground. I suppose the indiscriminate
contents of the Abbey, as well as its over-crowded-
ness (to which both living and dead contribute),
are its least attractive traits. However, it remains a
holy place, despite desecrations perpetrated by
Henry VIII and others, for there is the chapel of
St. Edward. That it was dedicated to St. Peter is
brought to mind at least on festivals, when St.
Peter's Flag, keys and all, is flown from one of
the great towers.

From a strictly architectural viewpoint, if you
can imagine the great building uncluttered, it is
truly splendid. The great vaulting, more French
than English in its proportions, is the second highest in England—three times as tall as it is wide.
The Henry VII Chapel, built between 1500-19, is
one of the most striking examples of late Perpendicular Gothic, with luxuriant fan vaulting, a
notably English architectural feature.

The present Houses of Parliament (officially
called the Palace of Westminster) are modern,
built in the middle nineteenth century, following
a disastrous fire. Westminster Hall is exceedingly
rich in history. Many trials were held here, among
them that of St. Thomas More. And here Richard
II was deposed.

While you are in the Westminster area, you may
wish to visit the Catholic cathedral, known as

Westminster Cathedral. It was built between 1895 and 1903, and like St. Louis Cathedral in Missouri is in a style that may be called Romano-Byzantine. You may be unimpressed by the exterior (the use of brick is not altogether happy), save for the 284-foot campanile (one of the best views in London may be seen from the top). On the other hand, it does harmonize with the brick structures of the district, and in style and texture it happily does not enter into competition with nearby Westminster Abbey or the more distant St. Paul's. Architect John F. Bently, building at a period when no contemporary style had developed, was wise in a choice that would not presume to rival the venerable Gothic and Renaissance manner of London's two established church buildings.

There is much here to make the Catholic feel at home: the atmosphere of prayer (this is no church-turned-into-a-museum), the stress on the Real Presence, artist Eric Gill's Stations of the Cross, the shrine of Blessed John Southworth, martyr, who died under Cromwell. If you are fortunate enough to be present at the Sunday Solemn Mass, you will very likely hear some of the finest choral music to be heard in any church.

St. Paul's, masterpiece of Sir Christopher Wren, was built after the Great Fire of 1666. The older building must have been very impressive indeed, with its spire taller than the present dome, even taller than the spire of Salisbury. The present structure will impress you as cool or cold, depend-

ing on your tastes. In the crypt is the modest grave
of Wren himself, with the famous epitaph: *Si
monumentum requiris, circumspice* ("If you seek
a monument, look around you"). However, one
scholar has pointed out that, if we recall the
trouble Wren had with the conservative building
committee that hampered his work, it is also "a
monument to the folly of those from whom Wren
suffered much." Others are buried there too—Van
Dyck, Turner, Millais and other painters—but, it
need hardly be said, no saints. One cannot escape
the feeling that this is more of a national monument, great as it is, than a house of God.

Among the holy places of London is, paradoxically, **the Tower,** really several buildings com-
prising a much-restored fortress. Within are two
former Catholic churches: St Peter-in-Chains
(where, in nameless graves, lie many martyrs'
bodies—St. Thomas More, St. John Fisher,
Blessed Margaret Pole and others) and the Royal
Chapel of St. John. The latter is one of the supreme jewels of early Norman architecture, as well
as a shrine of sacred memories. For it was there
that Blessed Edmund Campion, weakened by tor-
ture, stood and defended the Faith with such hero-
ism that the Earl of Arundel, Philip Howard, returned to the Faith and died for it. In the Tower
too you find images of the cross or of the Holy
Name, scribbled on the wall, before which many
martyrs prayed before going to judgment and
death.

Tyburn Tree stood near the present Marble

Arch; a triangular tablet in the middle of the street marks the spot. Like the Tower it is a place of immense horror and holiness, for here more than a hundred martyrs died for the Faith between 1535-1681, of whom the last was Blessed Oliver Plunket, Archbishop of Armagh. Although, as a historian has put it, "there is no more sacred spot in the land than this," no worthy monument celebrates it, and you will pray amid swirling traffic. However, a little way down Bayswater Road, a tiny Convent of Perpetual Adoration offers sanctuary, where you will want to stop and thank God for many things.

Another unlikely holy place (London is full of them), but one which you may *not* visit, is St. James' Palace, for long the official residence of the royal family (hence the phrase, "Court of St. James"). Here, in a private chapel belonging to the Duchess of York, in 1676 Blessed Claude La Colombière first preached the modern devotion to the Sacred Heart.

GALLERIES AND MUSEUMS

In art treasures London offers a difficult choice. Even if there are relatively few English creative artists of world rank, the island has produced many of the world's most discerning and acquisitive art collectors. London's museums are thus among the richest to be found anywhere. If you have time for only one, and your interest is painting, the one must be the **National Gallery** in Trafalgar Square.

Don't be dismayed by its drab, undistinguished, conventional exterior, a fate it shares with our New York Metropolitan and many other splendid museums, the beauties of which lie exclusively within. It offers surely one of the most representative collections in the world, with Da Vinci's "Virgin of the Rocks," Piero della Francesca's "Nativity," Michelangelo's "Entombment," Van Eyck's "Giovanni Arnolfini and his Bride," Constable's "Hay Wain," and as impressive a collection of Vermeer, Rembrandt, Ruisdael and Hals as you will find outside Holland—not to mention treasures of the Spanish, German, French and other schools. For British painting you will want to visit the Tate Gallery as well.

The **British Museum** is beyond description and requires many visits to make a dent in its enormous contents. Here one may see two of the most precious manuscripts of the Bible—the *Codex Sinaiticus* and the *Codex Alexandrinus,* as fresh and legible as when they were written, 1500 years ago. The Elgin Marbles, taken from the Parthenon, part of the finest collection of Greek sculpture in the world, and the Rosetta Stone (which gave the key to Egyptian hieroglyphics), are among the many treasures that make the British Museum a favorite among students of antiquity. Then there is an original copy of the *Magna Charta,* of *Alice in Wonderland,* a First Folio Shakespeare, and an incomparable collection of other books and manuscripts.

CATHEDRALS AND SHRINES

As you approach **Canterbury** in the south-eastern county of Kent, be sure to stop and visit St. Dunstan's Church, where you may venerate the head of St. Thomas More. Then move on to the great cathedral, the most venerable in all England, built on the site of St. Augustine's church, where the great missionary inaugurated the Christianization of the country, in 597. True, the Church had been in England earlier, possibly from early Roman times, but with the Saxon invasions it had become almost extinct. Before you leave Canterbury, make a short visit to nearby St. Martin's Church, part of which dates back to these pre-Augustinian days.

But the cathedral will occupy most of your time. Architecturally it is fascinating, incorporating most of the periods of English Romanesque and Gothic. The account of William of Sens, the architect who rebuilt the choir, 1175-1178, and how he was crippled in a fall from the scaffolding has been impressively dramatized by Dorothy Sayers in her *Zeal of Thy House,* which you will want to read. The cathedral contains many shrines, particularly those of St. Thomas à Becket (remember T. S. Eliot's *Murder in the Cathedral?*), St. Dunstan, St. Anselm, and the grave of Cardinal Pole, last Catholic archbishop of Canterbury. The shrine of St. Thomas à Becket was once resplendent, but it was desecrated under Henry VIII, who resented

anyone dead or alive that resisted royal authority
in matters spiritual. Today the worn pavement,
where pilgrims have trod, marks the spot of St.
Thomas' martyrdom more eloquently than any
shrine.

Not far from Canterbury is Rochester, where
St. John Fisher was bishop. It is not one of the
greatest cathedrals of England, but its connection
with the martyr makes it worth a visit.

In East Anglia, northeast of London, Norwich
cathedral is most impressive, in almost pure Norman style, with a lofty spire.

This Norfolk area has long had tender associations for Catholics, especially since the Dukes of
Norfolk have traditionally been known for their
fidelity to the Church. Not far from Norwich,
north and somewhat west, is a shrine that throughout the Middle Ages was dear to all Englishmen
and enjoyed an international reputation, that of
Our Lady of Walsingham. There, in 1061, just
five years before the Norman Conquest, Our Lady
appeared. From a simple wooden house, her shrine
grew immense and celebrated. Destroyed, of
course, at the Reformation, the site began to attract interest once again in 1921. The Anglicans
soon built a shrine, presumably on the spot of the
original, and the image of Our Lady was placed
there. The Catholics were able, however, to claim
the place known as the "Slipper Chapel," where
medieval pilgrims had begun the holy mile of
special prayer on their way to the shrine. The
Slipper Chapel is a restored fourteenth-century

building which was reconsecrated in 1938. Pilgrimages, both Catholic and Anglican, are carried out with great devotion and give hope that Our Lady of Walsingham may become influential in the movement of reunion, a goal for which all lovers of Mary devoutly pray.

Ely, much larger and more varied, is celebrated for its great length (521 feet) and the extraordinary central octagon over the crossing of nave and transepts.

To the north of Norwich, north and east of Ely, is **Lincoln,** one of the best known of English cathedrals, restored in pure Early English style by St. Hugh of Lincoln who directed its masterbuilder, Geoffrey de Noiers. The presbytery or "Angel Choir" has been called "one of the loveliest of human works." One may see one of the original copies of *Magna Charta* here too.

Farther north stands the great cathedral town of **York,** one of the supremely picturesque pilgrimage sites in England. York has kept much of its medieval atmosphere, with its fortress walls, winding streets, and many relics of its important past. The Cathedral Church of St. Peter—York Minster—is the largest, and one of the most beautiful of medieval English cathedrals. It covers the place of the baptism of King Edwin, ruler of Northumbria, by St. Paulinus (sent by Pope St. Gregory as missioner and first bishop of York), Easter Sunday, 627. York's antiquity and dignity account for its bishop being called, like that of Canterbury, "archbishop"—the only ancient Eng-

lish sees so honored. While the stained glass does
not compare with the finest in France, it is the
most striking collection to be found in England.
Among the many interesting sites to be visited in
York, do not miss the Bar Convent ("Bar" here
means "Gate"). Here many precious relics are
venerated, among them the hand of Blessed
Margaret Clitherow, a martyr at the time of the
Reformation.

Near York is a small cathedral at Ripon, which
you may see on the way to **Fountains Abbey,** one
of the most touching ruins in Britain. Fountains
was built at various periods from 1132 to 1526
(when the great tower was finished) to house the
largest Cistercian monastery in the country. The
chapel, in its dilapidated state, is still most impressive, particularly with the long transept at the east
side called the Chapel of the Nine Altars. Everything about Fountains will stir you, especially if
you have a chance to explore at twilight or under
an early morning fog.

While you are in this area, you will be well re-
warded by a visit to **Beverley,** a small market town
with two of the most imposing churches (not cathedrals) in Britain. The Minster ("minster" is
a corruption of the word "monastery") is greater
than many cathedrals, with its great towers, double
set of transepts and magnificent Percy Tomb, containing some of the finest of medieval sculpture.
St. Mary's, in a totally different style, rivals the
Minster in elegant statuary.

To the north, on the sea, are the famous ruins of

Whitby Abbey, of ecclesiastical and cultural history. Founded in 657 by St. Hilda, the abbey was for long the chief center of learning in Northumbria. It was here that the much-misunderstood Synod of Whitby was held in 664, to settle the question of the dating of Easter (the Celts had used an old method of calculating it, while Rome had changed in favor of a more accurate one; at Whitby it was decided that the Roman usage should be followed in Britain. A full account of the famous Synod can be found in Philip Hughes' *A History of the Church*).

This area is rich in the memory of seventh-century saints, among them St. Bede the Venerable, a most gracious person who salvaged much of ancient and Christian tradition; St. Benet Biscop, founder of great monasteries at Wearmouth and Jarrow (of which hardly a stone remains); St. Cuthbert of Lindisfarne ("Holy Island"), a monastery already founded by Irish monks from Iona.

Whatever you miss in England, make sure it is not **Durham,** a mammoth fortress of holiness and learning. In a commanding spot high on a peninsula of the Wear River are the great cathedral and the castle (now used by the university). When you enter the cathedral you will see what Dr. Johnson meant when he described it as "of rocky solidity and indeterminate duration," for it gives an impression of permanence and strength. It is an almost unparalleled example of fine Romanesque, while the Chapel of the Nine Altars (much like

that of Fountains Abbey) is in refined English
Gothic. The Galilee Porch contains the grave of
St. Bede the Venerable.

There is little to see in proverbially famous
Newcastle, but you may well take the drive toward **Carlisle** along the ancient Roman wall—
Hadrian's Wall, as it is called—seventy-three and
one-half miles of fortification built A.D. 122-126,
to hold back the barbarians of the North. Not
much of the Wall is still visible, but what there
is of it, as well as the vestiges of Roman roads
throughout Britain, reminds us visibly of what
great builders the Romans were. Carlisle has a
small, but sturdy cathedral and a castle from
which the view is excellent.

Now go northward into **SCOTLAND,** which
has been united (under the Crown) with England since 1603, when James VI of Scotland became James I of England. Since 1707 the Scots
have had no Parliament of their own, but have
sent members to Westminster. However, they remain very conscious of their own identity. In
1950, a group of zealots stole the Stone of Scone
(the coronation stone, originally Scottish, but now
used for the coronation of sovereigns of the United
Kingdom) from Westminster Abbey, a bold ges-
ture which reminded everyone that Scots are not
Englishmen.

Edinburgh, one of the handsomest and most
regal cities in Europe, delights in the title "Athens
of the North." True, it is grimy and has been given
the less complimentary sobriquet, "Auld Reekie"

("Old Smoky"), but it possesses the grandeur that one associates only with a capital city. Few cities anywhere can boast an avenue to match the dignity of Princes Street. As you climb the rock to visit Edinburgh castle, you enter the chapel of St. Margaret—now bereft of all but sacred memories. Still more poignant are the memories of Mary Queen of Scots, one of the most attractive characters in all history, as one visits the Palace of Holyroodhouse, where the tragic queen lived.

The church of St. Giles has been largely stripped of its beauty, thanks to the Puritanism of John Knox's followers. Much of the reformer's austere presence seems to abide in the city. His home may be visited at the foot of High Street. Not too far from Edinburgh is the spectacular Firth of Forth, and the picturesque ruins of Melrose Abbey.

Glasgow is a rather dismal industrial city, though it does boast the friendliest people and finest Gothic cathedral in Scotland, as well as a splendid art museum. However, a trip around Loch Lomond is rewarding, and there is a great deal to see if one wants the romantic beauty of the wild North. There are, too, attractive smaller cities with much tradition surrounding them: Perth, the ancient capital of Scotland; the home of golf, St. Andrews, and its university; Iona, of the Hebrides, the ancient shrine of St. Columba; Inverness, capital of the Highlands; Aberdeen, university city and resort; and many others.

Some miles southwest of Inverness, at the western end of Loch Ness, is old **Fort Augustus,** which dates back to the days of Bonnie Prince Charlie. In the last century a group of enterprising monks decided to establish an abbey here. It had been several centuries since the last Catholic priests had been seen in the area, but a number of clans that had kept the Faith during all this time slowly and somewhat skeptically accepted them as true priests. Much as the Japanese Christians, deprived of priests by persecution for several centuries, these old Scottish families had persevered in religious practices until the return of the clergy. The monks of Fort Augustus were the answer to their long, faithful prayers.

OTHER HISTORIC SITES

To the south of Scotland, bordered by England and the Irish Sea, lies rugged **WALES,** celebrated more for a romantic atmosphere than for monuments. North Wales boasts of Caernarvon Castle, some lovely villages, Mount Snowden (3,517 feet, the highest in England and Wales) and Tintern Abbey, famed through Wordsworth's poem—all surrounded by great natural beauty.

Coming back into **ENGLAND,** down the west side, be sure not to miss the Lake District, with its traditions of Worsdworth and Coleridge.

Preston, once the capital of the duchy of Lancaster, was and remains a center of Catholicism. Nearby Samlesbury Hall was once the home of the martyr, Blessed John Southworth, and the church there commemorates him. Lancashire's Whalley

Abbey, once splendid, now a touching set of ruins, recalls the "Pilgrimage of Grace" (you will want to refresh your memory by rereading Hilda Prescott's masterly novel, *The Man on a Donkey*—a work that evokes the tone of a complex and tragic moment in Church history.

Just four miles from Whalley is **Stonyhurst College,** one of the most historic and vital pivots of the Church in Britain. Founded in 1593 by Jesuits at St. Omer (Belgium) during the persecution under Elizabeth I, the college moved here in 1794. It uses a manor-house built in 1594-1606. The library is exceptionally precious, containing the famous *Cuthbert Gospel,* reckoned the oldest bound volume in the world, and relics of St. Thomas More (his seal and hat) and Mary Stuart's own prayer book.

Hurry past Liverpool if you can (unless you care to visit the new Anglican cathedral built by a Catholic architect, or the Catholic cathedral built by a Protestant). Then do spend some time in **Chester** (from the Latin *castra* or "camp") which still retains its walls and an enormous amount of charm. The walls, medieval as they are, are built where the Roman walls were; Foregate Street is the ancient Roman Watling Street. The old part of the city is rich in fine, old timbered houses. Colorful arcades called "Rows" link these buildings. The cathedral, built of red stone like that of Carlisle, is not large but contains many monuments within.

Continuing southward you will enter the region

of the Western cathedrals, each an individual gem
of architecture. We have not space to describe
them one by one, save to mention that Lichfield
(Dr. Johnson's home town), Shrewsbury, Here-
ford, Worcester, and Gloucester claim cathedrals
that any country would be proud to possess. A
happy renewal of Benedictine life (once so strong
throughout England and now again vigorous) you
will find if you visit Prinknash Abbey. This monastic group, which started on Caldey Island as
an Anglican foundation, came into the Church in
a body.

Somerset's **Bath, Wells** and **Glastonbury** form
a center of sacred tradition and art that must not
be missed. Bath is named after the ancient Roman
baths used from the first to the fourth century.
As a spa it has attracted Englishmen for many
years, and the houses, built in the eighteenth century on crescents, terraces and squares, are of rare
harmony. In some ways it is the handsomest town
in England. Be sure to see the Royal Crescent and
Prior Park with its preposterous "Romantic
Ruins." The present Abbey Church, on the site
of a monastery, is the last of the great English
pre-Reformation churches.

Wells is famous only for its cathedral, one of
the most original and surprising in England. Over
three hundred (there were four hundred before the
vandals went to work) statues adorn the main
façade, and several other views of the exterior are
equally rewarding. The interior too is full of un-

expected features, such as the immense inverted arch beneath the tower.

Just six miles away is Glastonbury, the ruins of whose Abbey are of striking loveliness. Legend has it that Joseph of Arimathea brought the chalice of the Last Supper (another legend says it was the vial containing the Sacred Blood of the Crucifixion) and founded a monastery here. St. Patrick is said to have visited Glastonbury and even to have died here. But what is certain is that Christianity and monasticism continued venerably at Glastonbury until suppressed in 1539 by Henry VIII.

You would do well, while in this neighborhood, to visit one of the leading post-Reformation Benedictine abbeys, Downside. Respected for its school and distinguished *Downside Review,* the monastery treasures its shrine of Blessed Oliver Plunket.

The Southwest too—Devon and Cornwall—has its sacred history, and fine cathedrals such as those of Exeter and Truro. However, if now you may choose but two more cathedrals, you have saved two of the finest till now. **Winchester** is the longest medieval church in all Europe, but its titles to glory are more significant. This was the original cathedral of the Kings of Wessex, enlarged in the ninth century by the famous St. Swithin, greatly rebuilt and further transformed by the famous bishops Walkelin, Waynflete and William of Wykeham. The great Norman transepts deserve

close study, and it is worthwhile to persuade the
sexton to escort you up into the triforium, where
you can feel their solid structure. In the choir are
great gilded mortuary chests containing the remains of King Canute, William Rufus and several
Anglo-Saxon monarchs. And do pay a brief visit
to Winchester College, founded in 1382 by Bishop
William of Wykeham. It is the oldest "public
school" in England. Among its famous students
the school names Sir Thomas Browne, Sydney
Smith, Thomas Arnold and Christopher Dawson.

If you have time to cross over to the Isle of
Wight, you will visit Quarr Abbey, rebuilt over
ancient ruins, and the center of some of the world's
finest sacred music in the Solesmes tradition.

There remains **Salisbury,** a classic of English
Gothic, and perhaps the most often pictured of
English medieval cathedrals, thanks especially to
Constable, who loved to sketch it. It is almost perfectly uniform in style, having been completed in
some forty years. Its great central spire (404
feet) climaxes the pyramidal structure with its
double transept. The interior is comparatively disappointing, owing to the unfortunate restorations
of various periods, but you may spend a whole day
viewing its great exterior from a hundred points.
Near the town of Salisbury are the ruins of Old
Sarum, a reminder of the ancient Sarum Rite (a
variation of the Roman Rite) which was used
throughout South England until the Reformation.

As you return to London you will want to stop

at Windsor, especially to visit the St. George
Chapel, one of the very finest examples of Tudor
Gothic, with elaborate fan vaulting. At hand too
is the verdant field of Runnymede, where King
John (very probably) sealed the Magna Charta in
1215, as well as Eton College, perhaps England's
most famous public school, and Beaumont, its
illustrious Catholic counterpart.

Near Salisbury you will not fail to visit one of
England's most ancient and most haunting monuments, though one that may prove disappointing
at first glance—**Stonehenge.** As you approach it,
especially if you arrive when the place is thronged
with tourists, you are not likely to be as impressed
as you expected to be. For one thing, outdoor
space never seems as large as enclosed space. Not
until you are within the great circle, preferably
alone or in a small company, will you feel its im-
pressiveness. Volumes have been written on Stonehenge and its mysterious origin and purpose. Its
careful orientation with reference to the sun suggests that it was a temple concerned with solar
worship. It seems also to have been, in part, a
sepulchral monument. There are two (now incom-
plete) circles, the inner one made of immense blue
stones brought all the way from Southern Wales
(the Preseli Hills). That such an undertaking was
accomplished suggests that these stones were
sacred. The date stipulated by a convergence of
astronomical and carbon calculations places Stonehenge some sixteen or seventeen hundred years

before Christ. It is thus the most ancient great structure in this part of the world, and long antedates the Druids.

The star attraction of the Midlands (though much overrated) is, obviously, **Stratford-upon-Avon,** celebrated as the birthplace of Shakespeare (1564). Since more than a hundred thousand tourists (mainly zealous Americans) visit Stratford annually, the town owes much of its prosperity to its great former citizen. The expected attractions are here: Shakespeare's house, Ann Hathaway's cottage, the school where Shakespeare is thought to have acquired his "little Latin and less Greek." There is the theater, where the plays are performed which many tourists feel they must attend. On the banks of the Avon is attractive Holy Trinity Church, which is itself well worth seeing, apart from Shakespeare's grave and the case containing his birth and burial certificates. The Harvard House will interest some Americans, since it was the house of John Harvard's mother; accordingly, members of Harvard University may visit the house free of charge while others pay sixpence.

The cathedral town of **Coventry** is not far north of Stratford, and I, for one, found it somewhat more interesting. The new cathedral, incorporating much of the finest in contemporary arts and crafts, is a worthy, if controversial, successor to the splendid building destroyed by bombing in 1940. By all means avoid nearby Birmingham, unless you have a special devotion to Cardinal Newman, who spent much of his life there, roughly from 1847, when he founded the Oratory of St. Philip Neri. Newman is buried on Rednal Hill, on the Bristol road.

OXFORD

The name of Newman quite naturally suggests the Oxford Movement, with which he was so closely associated. But, on many grounds, both the great universities must be included in your pilgrimage. We shall treat of the elder, Oxford, first.

"Towery city and branchy between towers . . . thou hast a brickish skirt," sang an eminent Oxonian of his university town. If Gerard Manley Hopkins found Oxford "brickish," we today find it more so. Superficially, the rather unattractive city has almost swallowed up the university (it has been waggishly said that Oxford is a university in a town, whereas Cambridge is a town in a university—which gives Cambridge some points, at least for the tourist). If Keats could no longer say today, "This Oxford, I have no doubt, is the fairest city in the world," many Oxonians surely continue to say, as Newman did, that "of all human things, Oxford is nearest my heart." But, enough of rhapsodies—on to Oxford, or rather, "up" to Oxford. One always goes "up" to Oxford or "down" from Oxford, whether to or from the North Pole or Mount Everest.

The center of the university is the set of buildings starting with St. Mary's Church on "the High" (the Oxford word for the High Street). It has a lofty (188-foot) spire, and you can begin your pilgrimage of Oxford best, I believe, by climbing to the balustrade of the tower and viewing the university as a whole. Newman was vicar here from 1828 to 1843, and an inscription to his memory and that of his friends and associates in the Oxford Movement (Keble and Pusey) will be found in the choir. Since the fourteenth century, at least, St. Mary's has been the official University Church, where select preachers (of whom Newman was probably the most famous) address the students.

Right back of St. Mary's are other buildings belonging to the university as such (it must be remembered that Oxford and Cambridge are federations of residential colleges, which own their own buildings and enjoy their own traditions and rivalries). One of these is the Radcliffe Camera, a handsome classical rotunda used as a reading room for the Bodleian Library. Another, the Bodleian (affectionately called "Bodley"), is the oldest and one of the most important libraries in the world, containing over forty thousand manuscripts. The Sheldonian Theatre (with its incredible, apparently unsupported ceiling) was built by Christopher Wren. Here honorary degrees and prizes are conferred. The Divinity School, built between 1430-80, boasts one of the noblest rooms anywhere, crowned by an astonishing fan vaulting and stone roof. Be sure to see it.

You are now facing Broad Street ("the Broad")
and will want to visit Trinity College (1555),
founded on the site of Durham College for Benedictine students. There is the Wren chapel—a
masterpiece on a modest scale—where Newman
prayed, and, facing the gardens, a bust that marks
his old quarters. Lord Baltimore, a founder of
Maryland, was another famous student of Trinity.
At Cambridge too you will see a Trinity College,
far larger and a few years older.

Next door is Balliol College, established in
1263, but whose buildings are, on the whole, Vic-
torian and dull. Among many famous members
were John Wyclif, Adam Smith, Cardinal Man-
ning, Arnold Toynbee and Hilaire Belloc. Just
back of Balliol is St. John's, founded in 1555, famous for its colonnades, its gardens, and Blessed
Edmund Campion. Just across St. Giles Street
you will see Blackfriars (the present Dominican
priory) and St. Benet's Hall (for Benedictines, and
part of the university), and Pusey House (a High
Church priory conducted by the Fathers of the
Resurrection, for Oxford is a center of Anglican
religious life).

The Ashmolean Museum has as great a collection of art and archeology as you would expect
such a university to possess, and farther down
Beaumont Street you will come to Worcester College (1714), formerly Gloucester College, general
house of studies for the Benedictines before the
Reformation, with its very attractive gardens and
some medieval cottages.

The southern part of Oxford is dominated by Christ Church (known familiarly as "the House"), founded in 1546. Cardinal Wolsey's, presence is still felt here. You may enter the great quadrangle ("Tom Quad") by the great Tom Tower, built by Wren, and if you are there at 9:05 in the evening you will hear the tower clock strike 101 times (one stroke for each member of the original school). Be sure to visit the great Hall, Oxford's largest and finest, where you will see portraits of eminent alumni of "the House": William Penn, John Locke, John Wesley, Gladstone, Ruskin, Pusey, Lewis Carroll, and others. St. Thomas More, too was a student where the Canterbury Quadrangle now stands. The cathedral (which is the chapel of Christ Church) is small but interesting, and has a modest shrine to St. Frideswide, who is reputed to have built a convent here in the eighth century. Before leaving, do stroll through Christ Church Meadow.

Across St. Aldate's, you may walk past Pembroke College (1624) (where Dr. Johnson was a student), down Brewer Street for a visit to Campion Hall (the Jesuit part of the university), an attractive modern building by Sir Edwin Lutyens. On St. Aldate's is Bishop King's Palace ("the Old Palace"), a handsome sixteenth-century house used as a student center for Catholics; this, of course, is where Monsignor Ronald Knox was chaplain.

Merton Street will bring you to Corpus Christi College (1516), with its fine early quadrangle, and to Merton College, one of the oldest now in existence (1264) at Oxford. Merton's chapel, library, hall and much else you will find worth visiting. As you walk north on Oriel Street you pass several quadrangles of Oriel College (1326), where Newman was a graduate fellow. His rooms are pointed out there, and a large statue of him is seen in the middle quadrangle.

This is a good place to re-enter "the High," which, with its graceful, gentle curve, is surely one of the most beautiful streets in England (despite the appalling traffic). You are again opposite St. Mary's, of course, and if you turn right you will visit All Souls' (1437), which is unique in having no undergraduates. The first quadrangle and chapel are especially worth visiting. Farther down are University College and Queen's College, both among the ancient parts of the university, though the buildings are predominantly seventeenth-century. The Shelley Memorial in University is gruesome and may be pleasantly bypassed.

Next we come to Magdalen (pronounced, as everyone should know, "maudlin"). Founded by William of Waynflete in 1448, it is in many ways the most beautiful college at Oxford. The great tower (145 feet, built 1492-1505, allegedly from designs by Cardinal Wolsey, who was then bursar in the college) gives a superlative view of the university. If you are there on May Day, early in the morning, you will hear the traditional hymn sung by Magdalen's superb choir, and afterwards witness much frolicking in the vicinity. Everything about Magdalen will delight you, especially as you stroll through the gardens and take Addison's Walk about the meadow.

Walk on the Long Wall Street toward the Old City Wall, and into New College (so called because founded in 1379). The buildings are much as their founder, William of Wykeham (who also founded Winchester College), left them, and form a superb ensemble. The chapel, with its ornate reredos, is perhaps Oxford's nearest rival to Cambridge's King's College chapel.

THE ENVIRONS

There are many other treasures of history and culture in the neighborhood of Oxford. Very likely you will want to visit nearby Littlemore, where Newman was received into the Church. His rooms are there, bleak and impressively austere, and the little church where he preached bears an inscription on the pulpit to "J.H.N." and has the original of "Lead, Kindly Light" framed on the wall. In terms of sheer charm, perhaps no small church in England can surpass Iffley, called the "best-preserved small Norman church in England." Just a few miles away is Dorchester Abbey, for many centuries the cathedral of this area, with some of the most exceptional medieval murals and stained glass in all England. The memory is here of St. Birinus, sent in 634 by Pope Honorius I, as apostle to this part of Britain.

CAMBRIDGE

Not far as the crow flies, but almost unreachable save by a long detour through London, is what in Oxford is called "the other place." No train service links Oxford and Cambridge, and even by bus you may bridge the impassable chasm only on week ends and bank holidays. Yet the two universities are more like each other than either is like any other place on earth.

Cambridge too has a St. Mary's, called "St. Mary's the Great," which serves as parish and university church. Nearby is the Senate House, which like the Sheldonian Theatre at Oxford, is used for university functions. Cross the Clare Bridge and enter King's College grounds, allowing yourself a good view of Cambridge's prized "Backs"—the banks of the River. You may visit the University Library, a modern structure containing a collection of books and manuscripts to rival that of the Bodleian Library. One of the richest treasures there is the *Codex Bezae,* a precious biblical manuscript.

King's College Chapel (built between 1446 and 1515) is a spectacular model of late Gothic, beautifully proportioned and with a rare collection of English stained glass. From the roof of the chapel, to the North, you enjoy a fine view of Ely Cathedral.

Queens' College, in Queens' Lane, founded in 1448, is one of the most attractive of both universities. Erasmus taught here, and his memory is kept by a "court" (the Cambridge equivalent of the Oxford "quad") and a tower. St. John Fisher was once president of this college.

Pembroke College, largely rebuilt since its foundation in 1347, has a fine chapel by Wren, and across Trumpington Street is Peterhouse, the oldest college in Cambridge, founded 1284. Just beyond is Fitzwilliam Museum, containing many fine English, French and other works of art. From the architectural point of view, you will find Jesus College (1496) especially fascinating. Built on the site of the convent of St. Radegund, it incorporates some of the old buildings, especially the interesting chapel.

The circular plan of the church of the Holy Sepulchre is unique. Parts of it date from 1130, others are later, but all have suffered from restoration. The nearby courts of St. John's College (1511) are exquisite examples of Elizabethan and Jacobean brickwork.

Then you come to Trinity College (1546), the largest in either university, with its seven hundred or so students, celebrated too for its great number of illustrious members, among them Dryden, Newton, Tennyson, Byron, Thackeray, Nehru. Nor does this, by any means, exhaust the manifold fascination of Cambridge.

You will find that a visit to the two universities is a journey through England's cultural history, from monastic foundations to the present. If in this abbreviated sketch of things to visit, despite my strenuous effort to be objective I have sounded partial to Oxford, put it down to the inescapable fact that I have *lived* there and explored its every nook and corner, whereas I have only *visited* Cambridge a few times. In each center of learning you will discover a microcosm of Britain and its pregnant past, as well as its unfailing present.

IRELAND

Of all the countries of Western Europe, Ireland is the hardest for the passionate pilgrim to write about, and, in some ways, the hardest to visit. Even if one is not at all Irish (is anyone "not at all Irish"?), or if, as I am, one is only fourth- or fifth-generation Irish, the pilgrim approaches the Isle of Saints with a blend of nostalgia and awe.

But apart from these sentiments, there is the problem of what to do. True, the Irish themselves were great pilgrims, and the ideal of "pilgrimage for Christ" played a large part in the spiritual lives of the Irish monks. Yet, on the whole, theirs was a pilgrimage *away* from Ireland, a missionary venture to bring Christ to the pagans, monasticism to Christians, and civilization to all. (If this begins to sound suspiciously like a St. Patrick's Day sermon, let me admit that these phrases belong to Arthur Kingsley Porter, Harvard Professor of Fine Arts, whose name and nationality absolve him of the charge of partiality, and whose work, *The Crosses and Culture of Ireland,* is a classic balance of objectivity and sympathy.)

Back to the problem of what to do. If one has come to Europe in quest of cultural monuments— Mont-Saint-Michel, Chartres and Ravenna, say— one may with little regret bypass Ireland altogether. As an exuberant Irish writer put it well, "in Ireland we have not yet had time to build monuments." Strange for a nation with such a long, close-knit cultural continuity.

The truth is more complex. Professor Porter puts it well when he points out that "modest architecture was in accordance with the ideals of asceticism and austerity for which the Irish Church was celebrated." Irish culture grew up outside the pale of the Roman Empire and its ancient cities. True, there were palaces, at Tara for example, and rather immense monasteries at a later period. Several of these, such as Boyle Abbey, Jerpoint and Mellifont, will remind you of the great British monasteries in their poignant ivy-clad state of ruin.

Indeed, it is a truism that need not be belabored here, that the Irish suffered incalculably for their Faith and their Irishness. Few countries have been allowed to preserve a smaller share of buildings that housed the most treasured institutions. Many a shrine has had to be rebuilt in modern times, after the Emancipation, following wholesale destruction by foreign iconoclasts.

Most of us visitors (a word the Irish prefer to use for us rather than the distasteful "tourist") to Ireland find, nonetheless, much to admire and even more to love. The emeraldness of the Island strikes you even more intensely than you expected from the cliché—whether you first sight it, as I did, from a ship's porthole in Cobh; or, as I did the second time, going around the coast of Donegal in the North. And the impression lasts. Few Western countries have preserved, even after millennia of civilization, such a treasury of untouched natural scenery. There are lakes, even today, by which you spy hardly a house, hardly a boat, hardly a human being. All like the very day of Creation.

Then, when one has begun to come into contact with the real Irish themselves (I shall not make bold to say with whom I am contrasting the "real Irish"), one notes their affinity with the landscape. They seem as unspoiled as the verdant countryside. Their charm is, of course, proverbial, and the proverb proves to be right. Innocent of time and in no way miserly of it, they gladly give as many minutes as you are disposed to allot, answering your questions, sharing your sentiments. The legend about the Blarney Stone is well founded, even if not literally true. Eloquence is part of the Irish heritage, whether that of oratory or of conversation.

DUBLIN

If you fly in from America, you may land in Shannon and start your visit from there, or you may want to go right on to Dublin, just an arc away in the plane's trajectory. You will instantly note that the country is physically small, much smaller than our western, midwestern or southern states. If you come by ship, you will very likely land in Cobh. Or if you are already in Europe, you will dock at Dublin. In any case, Dublin, the capital, is an essential part of your visit.

Dublin is more than the capital; it holds a fourth of the nation's population. Many, especially the British, are disappointed, to find the city so British. After all, they should remember, their ancestors made it so. There is some of the faceless grayness that characterizes unsightly places like Leeds, Birmingham, Manchester, Glasgow and Liverpool. But with a difference. For one thing, Dublin is a *capital* city, and capitals have a grandeur—even when, as in Washington, Brussels or Madrid, one would like to forget unspeakable slums and the repetitiousness of governmental architecture.

From the architectural viewpoint, Dublin is largely an eighteenth-century city; it would be hard to find a more distinguished assembly of Georgian houses anywhere (except, perhaps, in Bath) than along Fitzwilliam Place, just off Lower Leeson Street. Elegance, dignity, the eighteenth century par excellence are concentrated here, as on or near Merrion Square, where a number of national buildings are impressively grouped: the National Library, the National Gallery of Art, the National Museum (with a superb collection of ancient Irish art), and others. In the same area, and in roughly the same style of architecture, is **Trinity College,** its entrance flanked by statues of Oliver Goldsmith and Edmund Burke.

Trinity is, of course, of greater interest to foreigners than to the Irish, who recall that it was founded in 1591 by Elizabeth I on a spot where the Monastery of All Hallows had been, until suppressed by Henry VIII. But on the roster of its alumni are many illustrious Anglo-Irish—Goldsmith, Burke, Swift, Congreve, Berkeley and others. Whatever his affections or disaffections for this phase of Ireland's life, the visitor will enjoy the Trinity quadrangles, and especially the library. It too is eighteenth-century, having been started in 1712, and its contents are celebrated. *The Book of Kells*—possibly the most famous and probably the most beautiful book in the world—is there, a seventh-century copy of the gospels, with illuminations that show Irish art at its peak. This art was to be carried to England and the Continent, but nowhere is it more exquisitely achieved than here. *The Book of Durrow* and that of *Armagh,* also in the library, are among the treasures of Irish history and craftsmanship.

You will note again the paradox of Dublin when you visit the two cathedrals (both Anglican now). **Christ Church Cathedral** (the ancient Priory Church of the Holy Trinity—devotion to the Holy Trinity having always been especially strong in Ireland) dates back to 1038, but it has been rebuilt and altered many times since. Its ancient crypt contains a number of tombs, one of them supposedly that of "Strongbow," who in 1172 began a new church on the site. **St. Patrick's Cathedral** was built over the Well of St. Patrick, where the saint is said to have baptized. It is a large, stately structure, chiefly in Early English style, with a 221-foot steeple. Jonathan Swift was dean here; his tomb may be seen not far from the entrance.

Paradoxically, Dublin's religious life is seen, however, not in ancient churches, for all their historic interest. The Catholic **Metropolitan Pro-Cathedral** (a modest and almost ironic title—for the overwhelming majority of the Irish belong to the Catholic Church, and not to the Church of Ireland), conceived in heavy Doric style, is rather inconspicuously placed on Marlborough Street. It is, nevertheless, a true center of piety. There is, one senses, in Irish Catholicism, something of the atmosphere of a church just emerged from the catacombs. A traditionalist eclecticism seems to have dominated most church building until quite recently, when a fresh, agreeable, breath of the modern has been felt in Donegal, Cork, Limerick and some other spots.

Before leaving Dublin, you will probably attend a performance or two of the Abbey Players (soon to be resituated in their theater, after a fire forced them to take up temporarily in Queen's Theatre). You will be amazed, perhaps, at the variety and vitality of the theater in such a small city, until you recall the number of Irish and Anglo-Irish playwrights that have frequently invigorated "English" drama. Indeed, has any country produced so many important writers in anything like the same proportion as Ireland?

THE PILGRIMAGES

Before going into the pilgrimages *in* Ireland, we ought to reflect on the pilgrimages *from* Ireland. The prolific French writer, Henri Daniel-

Rops, has compiled an enlightening volume that should be read by anyone interested in Ireland's place in history—*The Miracle of Ireland,* a work of the "high popularization" that the French do so well. Despite its title, the book is written almost entirely by non-Irishmen with no axe to grind.

"The monasteries founded by St. Patrick," contributor Georges Goyau informs us, "were mission stations . . . Scarcely were they baptized when the Irish wished to become monks . . . in order to preach, to bring about more baptisms and to produce more monks." The number and influence of these missionary-monks is almost incalculable. We discover St. Comgall founding a monastery in Chester, England; St. Ninian founding one in Scotland; St. Columba establishing the monastery of the island Iona, which was to be a "nursery of bishops," from which Christianity would reach even Iceland; St. Brendan evangelizing the Atlantic Communities, perhaps even the New World; any number of Irish monks establishing monasteries in Brittany and other parts of France; others going across the Rhine and Alps, down even into Italy, where Bobbio, one of the greatest monasteries of the world became the resting place of the redoutable St. Columban. One of Columban's disciples, St. Gall founded the celebrated monastery of Switzerland, which for centuries would be a fountain of sanctity and culture. We find even the Englishman, Venerable Bede, paying homage to the culture of the Irish monks. We know too that the Carolingian Renaissance owed

much to their intellectual influence. M. Daniel-
Rops asks whether even "our countries would
have been Christian" at all without "the Irish
Miracle."

We do not know precisely when or how Christianity began in Ireland. St. Patrick, to whom so
much was due, was not the first to preach Christ
there, any more than St. Augustine was the first
in England. Pope Celestine I had sent a missionary
called Palladius as bishop "to govern those who
already believe in Christ." But from 432 onwards,
another name dominates Irish Catholicism, Patrick, a Briton by birth (it seems now established),
a former slave in Ireland and a traveler in France.
Patrick's death seems to have occurred about the
year 461, and though the shamrock legend begins
long after this, we know that he had implanted in
Ireland an abiding love for the Holy Trinity and
for Christ. "Christ with me, Christ before me,
Christ behind me, Christ in me, Christ beneath
me, Christ above me, Christ on my right, Christ
on my left, Christ in breadth, Christ in length,
Christ in height," he sang in the great hymn called
"St. Patrick's Breastplate."

St. Patrick left a legacy of tough, uncompromis-
ing Christianity. Irish monks developed a tradition
of austerity that makes us shudder. Even today,
after centuries of persecution and hardship, Irish
Catholics love to make pilgrimages to the holy
places, under conditions that make softer Americans hesitate to join. The pilgrimage to **Lough
Derg** in Donegal, for example (variously called

St. Patrick's Purgatory or Station Island), is admittedly "the most rigorous in Christendom." Three days of almost absolute fasting and strenuous barefoot penitential exercises are expected of the tens of thousands who make it annually. This spot (according to D.D.C.P. Mould, whose authoritative *Irish Pilgrimage* is eminently readable) "certainly has nothing to do with St. Patrick." Lough Derg's origins as a shrine are lost in obscurity, but throughout the Middle Ages it grew in popularity as a place where sinners from all Europe would come to do penance. During the persecutions that came with the Reformation, Lough Derg became "a symbol and rallying point for the Irish Catholics"; today it is their principal shrine of pilgrimage. It is something of a symbol of the Church's universality that in the shop there one may buy, not statues of Irish saints, but of St. Martin de Porres, the Negro South American.

Perhaps not quite as grim, but still terrifyingly demanding by American standards, is the pilgrimage to County Mayo's **Croagh Patrick,** the holy mountain where St. Patrick spent all Lent of the year 441 in prayer and fasting for the Irish. On the last Sunday of July each year some eighty thousand people climb the mountain in prayer, often barefoot. Smaller group pilgrimages take place at other times too. The Celtic saints, steeped in Scripture, which so often speaks of holy mountains, loved to go up into the mountains to pray. Often too they found pre-Christian holy places, which they would exorcize and christen, sensing in them no intrinsic evil. They considered them part of God's creation that could and should fit into the religion of Him who came to fulfill, not to destroy. A competition was held in 1958 for a design for an oratory to be built on Croagh Patrick. The plans of architect Patrick J. Quinn awarded first prize are reproduced in the special issue of *Liturgical Arts* magazine dedicated to Irish art (August, 1961). The design is in keeping with the ascetic nature of the place. Local stone is used in a traditional way and does offer shelter against prevailing winds. Nothing will be done, however, to soften or otherwise harm the spirit of penitential pilgrimage.

Dr. Mould does not mention in her book the pilgrimage that bids fair to becoming Ireland's most popular. Not too far from Croagh Patrick, also in County Mayo, in 1879 occurred an apparition of the Blessed Virgin in the parish church of **Knock.** The vision was witnessed by a number of people and has been investigated by the Church. The shrine's popularity grew and grew, in keeping with the Marian devotion of our time. Today some two hundred thousand pilgrims visit Knock annually. Here there is little of the hardness and rigor of the ancient Irish holy places; rather, the mood is one of tenderness and confidence in Our Lady, to whom the Irish traditionally have been dedicated.

In connection with the Irish shrines, it is interesting to find several local customs that are traditional and that might be called "folk liturgy."

Recognizing that man is both body and soul, the Irish have found ways of praying that assert the fact. One is the "rounds" that seem to go with shrines, great or small. You do not only approach the holy place, but walk around it, in what are called "right-handed sunwise circles." This "liturgical movement" (as a wag called the custom) has the advantage of keeping crowds circulating. Besides, how else can everyone share the sacred object?

Another tradition is that of the Pattern (doubtless a corruption of the word "patron"), during which prayers are counted by a handful of pebbles; at the end of each "Our Father" or "Hail Mary" one pebble is thrown away.

Ireland is dotted with vestiges of holy places—holy wells, stones, and round towers, and especially holy Celtic crosses. No single one of them, perhaps, will attract the casual visitor for long. But their great profusion throughout the country are reminders of holiness reaching past the penal days into time immemorial. One spot, close to Dublin and easily reached, is a "must"—the remains of **Glendalough** (literally "Glen of Two Lakes"). Here during the Middle Ages a specified number of pilgrimages (seven, in fact) were deemed the equivalent of one to Rome. This may have been so thought because sixth-century St. Kevin was said to have brought there bits of Roman earth. The Irish loved (and love) to bury their dead near such holy places. (Since little bits of Rome were placed in burial grounds, cemeteries were called "roms.") The round tower is especially fine at Glendalough, as is the unspoiled wildness of the area.

More remote, indeed almost inaccessible, is craggy **Skellig Michael** off the coast of Kerry. Rising bleak as a spike, seven hundred feet above the ocean, was a monastery as far back as the seventh century; when or why it was deserted, we do not know. Its natural setting is even more impressive than another rock of St. Michael's—Mont-Saint-Michel—but there is not the consummate work of centuries of monks that serves to make the French monastery so humanly splendid. Here, rather, all is stark even if majestic. Nearby you will see the heavy masonry of the monks and their fearsome beehive cells.

Another imposing ruin is that of **Cashel** in Tipperary, once the residence of the kings of Munster, but given to the Church in 1101, by King Mortaugh, who moved the capital to Limerick. An effective chapel, said to have been Cormac's, is one of the glories of Irish architecture during the Romanesque period. Not too far is **Clonmacnoise,** where Cormac's enemy, King Flann, had a great cross, which is now much studied by scholars. Here on the River Shannon, one of the greatest of Irish monasteries and schools attracted scholars came from foreign countries. Apart from the two impressive round towers, all is destruction, as we find so often in Ireland, but the ruins evoke a deep, rich past.

One more cross and one more set of ruins must

be mentioned: In ruined **Monasterboice,** you will read on a monolithic cross in ancient Irish, the inscription: "A prayer for Muiredach by whom was made the cross." It seems to date from about the year 900. Filled with interesting scriptural sculpture, the cross is an object of veneration and study. Dr. Porter, for example, includes several photographs of every detail of the great cross, and gives some fifteen pages to an analysis of the sculpture found on it.

There is much else to see in Ireland—spots fabled in song and story. There are the Killarneys, as lovely as their name and fame are fair. There is Armagh, primatial see of Ireland, where St. Patrick did so much, but where so little of him remains. Galway, which may be the most beautiful in the island, and poetic Connemara and the Aran islands. And castles, new and old, each with their yarns and legends. And, more important, the humble little holy places, such as Gallerus Oratory, that go back to St. Patrick's day; and Mount Melleray, where today's Trappists live lives of prayer and privation, at one with Ireland's ancient hero-saints.

GERMANY

Anyone who has been in Germany recently and remembers what it was like right after World War II, hardly hesitates to use the expression that has become hackneyed—"the Miracle of West Germany." If it were not for a number of scars still evident, it would be hard to believe the destruction of the last great holocaust. Surely "the Miracle" is something unique in human history. It is all too easy to say, "Oh, look at all the aid we gave them." If American aid was prodigious, how much more extraordinary is the use made of it in this land of industry and tireless work.

Accordingly, you could easily concentrate your visit on the strictly contemporary: the modern city planning, new industrial techniques, postwar architecture. **Berlin,** which previously was not known as a particularly interesting city in terms of architecture, is now a world center for it. The Hansa Viertel, for example, is an amazing collection of buildings done by masters Gropius, Le Corbusier, Aalto, Niemeyer and others. While it has been criticized for some lack of unity, the Hansa is well worth seeing and studying. For if, as G. E. Kidder Smith notes in his study *The New Architecture of Europe,* German architecture has not been as progressive as French or Italian, the reason may be

171

that "the German architects have been so busy
building that they have not had time to think."

Yet, for church architecture the contemporary
Germans are hard to match. Take St. Anna
(Dueren), or Christ Church (Leverkusen-Buerig),
or St. Albert (Saarbruecken), for instance, and you
will be hard put to find anything more satisfying.
Or Trinity Church (Mannheim), with its wonderful glass by Gabriel Loire of Chartres (whose work
we now find everywhere from there to the Colo-
rado College for Women chapel in Denver). Concert halls too have been elegant and imaginatively
experimental, as one might expect in the land that
for almost two centuries gave the world most of
its best music. I was impressed, for example, by
the new opera house in Cologne as well as by the
concert hall in Stuttgart.

West Germany (technically, of course, The
Federal Republic of Germany) is roughly the size
of Oregon, and even without West Berlin has a
population of some fifty-five million. It is by no
means homogeneous, in any recognizable way.
Not only are different dialects spoken, in addition
to official German; but there are heavily industrial
areas, especially in the North, where population
density averages more than a thousand per square
mile. In the picturesque agricultural and mountain areas, the population will average only a
third as much.

Much of West Germany (the part that we associate roughly with the Rhineland) was once part
of the Roman Empire. It is a curious fact that

the borders of West Germany correspond very
closely, on the East, with those of Charlemagne's
empire (which also included France, Benelux,
Switzerland, Austria, and Italy down almost as far
as Naples).

From the historical and Christian-Humanist
viewpoints, the most interesting parts of West
Germany tend to be concentrated along the Rhine,
the Weser and the Danube rivers, and, of course,
in Bavaria. A map of great churches, however,
would group them interestingly according to period
and style: while the Rhineland tends to be Gothic
and Romanesque, and the Weser country largely
Romanesque, Bavaria and the Danube are the
land of the baroque.

THE SHRINES

The shrine, par excellence, of Germany, where
the bishops gather annually at the grave of the
apostle of Germany, is, of course, **Fulda,** in central
Germany some seventy-odd miles from Frankfort. Paradoxically, the apostle, St. Boniface, was
an Englishman. This fact should remind us of
what Christopher Dawson points out: that England's greatest export has been saints. The monastery St. Boniface had founded here in 744 became, in turn, a radiating source of spiritual and
cultural energy which sent great abbots and scholars to all parts of the medieval German world.
Following the destructive Thirty Years War
(1618-1648), during which Fulda and all of

Germany suffered incalculably, the city built up importantly once again and is now predominantly a baroque city.

Another shrine of immense historical significance is near the borders of Belgium and Holland. In Charlemagne's day, the capital of the world (the Western World that is) was **Aachen.** That Charlemagne's grave was there later inspired kings, emperors and other rulers of Germany to want to be crowned there. No fewer than thirty-two Holy Roman Emperors, in fact, did come here for their coronation. The French name for Aachen (Aix-la-Chapelle) tells the two things for which it is famous: "Aix" is a corruption of the Latin for "waters"—Aachen's springs are the hottest in this part of the world as well as the most historical; "la Chapelle" refers to the great chapel, part of the complex cathedral, in which Charlemagne is buried.

The interesting octagonal dome of the chapel will remind you of the church of San Vitale, in Ravenna, another royal city. There is no question that it is an imitation of San Vitale. Indeed some of the columns were brought here from Ravenna and Rome.

Charlemagne's "throne," the treasury and the shrine of Our Lady have made this the "most famous place of pilgrimage north of the Alps." In addition, Aachen has an exceptional museum of wood sculpture from the twelfth century to the eighteenth, as well as an exceptional painting collection.

South of Aachen flows the Moselle river, celebrated thousands of years ago by the Roman poet
Ausonius in delightful verse. Where it and the Saar
and Ruwer meet is the ancient Roman city of **Trier**
(Trèves, in French). The Porta Nigra ("Black
Gate") is a monumental piece of Roman architecture of which the natives are rightly proud. "Rome
itself has no Porta Nigra," they are heard to boast.
You will also see ancient Roman baths and an
amphitheater, the cathedral, one of the oldest
churches in Germany, the church of Our Lady and
baroque St. Paulinus' church.

Farther north and on the Rhine, **Cologne** is a
glorious city, and, together with Trier and Mainz,
a contender for the title of most ancient city in
Germany. Like Rotterdam it is a "phoenix" city,
having risen miraculously from its ashes. The
cathedral, nearly five hundred feet in length and
crowned by towers that rise even higher, is one
of the largest and most exciting in the world.
While from a strictly architectonic viewpoint it
is possibly not as original as Amiens (which it imi-
tates), it remains overwhelming, having survived
the city's destruction. In its treasury are shrines
of many German saints.

Also in Cologne are several other famous
churches, among them the basilica of St. Pantaleon, that of St. Gereon with its ten-sided nave,
and the rebuilt churches of St. Peter and St. Cecilia. Beyond St. Pantaleon is a venerable church,
where St. Peter Canisius preached, now the prop-
erty of the Evangelical Church. And there are

memories here of the great St. Bruno, founder of
the Carthusians, who was born in Cologne.

While in this neighborhood, you may go north
to Düsseldorf and its interesting shrines; to the
world at large, however, the city is best known as
the home of Heine, Goethe, Brahms and the
Schumanns.

South of Cologne lies **Bonn,** capital of West
Germany, an ancient Roman city, celebrated also
as the birthplace of Beethoven. The basilica, with
its octagonal tower 308 feet high, is a very fine
example of Rhineland Romaneseque. Several modern churches will prove interesting too, as well
as the new Beethoven Hall.

Coblenz is particularly rich in Romanesque
churches. Near it is a monastery that has played
a large part in the life of Christendom from 1093
to the present. Very picturesque, with its typical
towers, Maria Laach has been quite contemporary
in its liturgical developments, especially under the
leadership of Abbot Ildefonse Herwegen.

You are expected to take a Rhine trip at some
point. A particularly good one runs from Coblenz
to Mainz, with castles galore, matchless towns,
and, of course, the Lorelei, the tall cliff and dan-
gerous narrows, the Lorelei of classic myth.
Speyer's cathedral of St. Mary and St. Stephen is
the largest Romanesque church in Germany, perhaps in the world. Nine emperors are buried here,
in a very moving crypt.

Where the Rhine meets the Neckar is Mannheim, a great cultural center, famed for its or-

chestra and orchestral tradition which had so
much to do with developing classical symphonic
music. Wiesbaden nearby is celebrated for recrea-
tion and for its May Festival of opera, theater and
ballet.

Across the Rhine is **Mainz,** "the Golden City,"
built by the Romans c. 38 B.C. St. Boniface became, in 745, the first archbishop of Mainz, which
remained central in the politics of the medieval
Holy Roman Empire. St. Martin's Cathedral, begun in 975, is a remarkable example of Romanesque, with later additions harmoniously made.
Here Gutenberg lived, and invented printing as
we know it. The university, appropriately, has
been renamed after him.

THE ROMANTIC ROAD

To the south we enter what is often called
"Romantic Germany." The river Neckar is full
of legend and crowned by **Heidelberg,** the great
German university town. Don't expect it to be
another Oxford or Salamanca. Its beauty is altogether different. Yet the atmosphere seems almost too romantic to be true—the castle high in
the hills, with a wonderful view of the valley and
outdoor festivals in the summer, the narrow winding streets, several superb churches.

Moving to the southeast, you will find **Ulm,**
on the Danube. Ulm is an ancient walled city,
with gates and towers still standing. The Gothic
cathedral is elegant, with the tallest tower in the

world, 528 feet (so it is said, a fact hard to prove
or disprove; much depends on your definition of
"tower"). The fifteenth-century Gothic choir stalls
by Jörg Syrlin the Elder are considered the finest
in Germany. Ulm, in modern times, is famous as
the birthplace of Einstein.

Another wonderful city of the South, which
claims the most beautiful tower (it is only 380
feet high) is **Freiburg-im-Breisgau** (not to be confused with Fribourg in Switzerland), an ancient
cathedral and university town with gracious
squares and picturesque inns. This is the area of
the Black Forest, so called from its dark ever-
greens.

In the old principality of Hohenzollern (from
which the former ruling house of Prussia came),
on the Danube and just about midway between
Freiburg and Ulm, is the archabbey of **Beuron.**
Founded in 1077, suppressed during the Napole-
onic era in 1803, re-established by monks from
St. Paul's-outside-the-Walls in Rome, since the
late nineteenth century it has been a pivot of the
liturgical and artistic life of the Church. Beuron
art and Beuron chant are now world famous; and
even if some of us find them a bit stiff, there is
no gainsaying their dignity.

Lake Constance is worthy of its reputation.
From the pilgrim's viewpoint, its most interesting
feature is Reichenau Island, where the great
Benedictine abbey was a world-famous center of
piety and culture. There are three splendid Romanesque churches on the island. And Constance

itself was the seat of the sixteenth Ecumenical Council (1414-1418).

"The Romantic Road" is a picture-book trip through one of the most enchanting parts of Europe. You will see the incredible Neuschwanstein castle (really built only in the last century by the mad Ludwig II of Bavaria).

Augsburg, however, is real and genuine, and will appeal to all of your cultural interests. Dating back to ancient Roman times, it has been associated with the Mozart family, Martin Luther, Holbein the Elder, and the famous family of prince-merchants, the Fuggers. Its cathedral claims the oldest stained glass in the world, and its Renaissance tone has given it the title of "City of the German Renaissance." At the end of "the Romantic Road" is another ancient town, Würzburg, famous for its Cathedral of St. Kilian (restored after much wartime destruction), its charming eleventh-century church of St. Burkard, and a remarkable baroque castle.

Turning south and east, on the way to Munich, you will enjoy a visit to **Nuremberg** and **Regensburg** (Ratisbon), both magnificent centers of German Gothic. Despite immense destruction during the war, Nuremberg has been skillfully rebuilt to retain much of its attractiveness. Here were the Meistersingers, celebrated in Wagner's exciting music-drama; here too are the famous Germanic Museum and the St. Lawrence and St. Sebald churches, all late medieval, during the transitional period between Gothic and Renaissance.

Nearby, at Bayreuth, you may wish to visit the Wagner shrine and possibly attend the Wagner festivals, if you are fortunate enough to have arranged for tickets. Try to forget about Hitler, who tried to exploit Nuremberg in terms of the crudest nationalism. Regensburg's Cathedral of Peter, with its superlative twin towers, rivals that of Cologne. The town itself was founded in the time of the Romans.

MUNICH

Munich is recognized as the art capital of Germany. Not only does it contain exceptionally rich museums, but the whole city has the flavor—only in the good sense, however—of a living museum. Indeed, Munich's *Gemütlichkeit,* always evident, overflows especially at *Fasching* (Mardi Gras) and *Katzenjammer* (around Christmas), when the city seems a very boisterous museum indeed.

Among Munich's galleries, the Bavarian State Art Museum (once called "Old Pinakothek") is to German painting what the Prado is to Spanish. Its Dürers and Cranachs can hardly be matched elsewhere, and, if we except the Rijksmuseum, much the same can be said of its Flemish and Dutch masters. Rembrandt's "Deposition," "Crucifixion" and "Ascension" are clearly among that master's most gripping, profound sacred works. Of the Italians, Titian's superb "Christ Crowned with Thorns," a masterwork of his extreme old age, and Raphael's "Madonna dei Tempi," a very satisfying work by a great master who sometimes disappoints, add to the supreme quality of the collection.

The Frauen-Kirche cathedral, with its onion domes, offers an interesting use of brick in Gothic (sometimes decried by those purists who suppose that Gothic has to be in stone). The church of St. John Nepomuk, in rococo style, harmonizes well with the general mood of the city, showing a bewitching sense of movement and excitement in its lines. Half a dozen other baroque and rococo churches will, perhaps, widen your sense of Catholicism, as you see its particular Bavarian manifestation.

Munich is coming to be known as the city of Father Rupert Meyer, one of the leading spiritual heroes of our century. Father Meyer, who courageously resisted the Nazis, is buried in a crypt-chapel in St. Michael's church, where he developed his model men's sodality. It is hoped that before long he will be canonized.

OTHER CITIES

In a country as diversified as Western Germany it is hard to make a selection, since each region has its own color and tradition. Frankfort, in the center, is bursting with modernity and vigor. The great northern cities, too, are rich in interest of all sorts. Take Lübeck, for example, its cathedral and the Marien-Kirche, with its unforgettable Romanesque brickwork, which dates back to the thirteenth century. Münster's cathedral of St. Peter and St. Paul is only one of that city's glories. And there is Hamburg (with its rich Kunsthalle, superb new Barlach Museum and much contemporary architecture) and Hanover and many other bustling industrial cities, built on age-old traditions. Indeed, few countries offer such contrasts of success and tragedy; old and new; technology and fine arts; scientists, cynics, saints.

AUSTRIA

Austrians like to think of their tiny little country as the heart of Europe, and there is, for most of us, an ironic poignancy in the thought. Less than thirty miles from Vienna, at the border of Hungary lie the limits of freedom. Yet, for centuries Vienna was a crossroads between East and West, North and South, with something of all. No city used to be more cosmopolitan. It was the Paris of Central Europe.

VIENNA

Such glory is now, of course, only a sad memory; nevertheless, Vienna manages to remain anything but sad. Its inhabitants, freed from military occupation, have returned to the proverbial gaiety, charm, *Gemütlichkeit* that make Vienna one of the most attractive cities in all Europe. Even apart from Vienna, Austria, small though it is, is a country rich in people and in beauty. It now advertises itself as "the ideal vacation land." It is surely that, though one wonders how wistfully the older inhabitants may look back to a period when Vienna was the center of a vast, diverse and glamorous empire.

Dominating Vienna's skyline is the Stefansdom ("St. Stephen's Cathedral"), now reconstructed to its former glory, one of the most soaring and impressive of cathedrals. Try to attend at least one High Mass there, or at the Hofburg Chapel (where the Vienna Boys Choir sings every Sunday morning at 9:30), and you will understand the meaning of Haydn's and Mozart's Masses. These magnificent compositions, ornate as they are, seem unliturgical elsewhere; but here, *in situ,* they appear perfectly in place, expressing the majesty and glory of God.

The cathedral tells something of the history of Vienna. The west front and some other parts are Romanesque, dating back to 1147; the choir and nave are late Gothic; the single tower (the other left unfinished because of religious disunity) was completed in 1433; yet the altars are almost all baroque, and a baroque feeling somehow imposes itself on the whole interior.

The Peterskirche, though much older, having roots in Roman times, was completely rebuilt in the baroque era. St. Maria am Gestade is famous for the preaching of St. Peter Canisius and for St. Clement Mary Hofbauer, who was instrumental in saving it. His altar should not be missed. The Karlskirche (St. Charles Borromeo) is a superlative baroque structure; nearly every detail will remind you of Rome. In the crypt of the Capuchin Church, the burial place of the royal Hapsburg family, you will find the graves of many persons famous in history.

The Ringstrasse, built over the ancient ramparts of Vienna, one of the most striking streets in Europe, will give you a chance to view several of Vienna's finest buildings: the Parliament, part of the Hofburg, the Rathaus, the Opera House and a number of museums. Of the latter, allow some time to visit at least the Kunsthistorisches ("Fine Arts") Museum, where Brueghel's most famous works (such as "Peasant Dance") are to be found, together with excellent works of Velázquez (second only to the Prado), Titian, Tintoretto, Rubens and the German masters. For engravings by the great masters—Michelangelo, Holbein, but especially Dürer—no museum anywhere can match the Albertina. In prehistoric finds the Naturhistorisches ("Natural History") Museum is truly exceptional, with its famous "Venus of Willendorf" (perhaps the oldest of artistic statues in the world) and many objects of the Hallstatt period.

As you would expect in the world's most illustrious music capital, there are many museums of manuscripts of Beethoven, Mozart, Schubert, Haydn, Bruckner and other composers who made Vienna their home. And no music lover needs to be reminded of the stature of Vienna's opera and several symphony orchestras.

Vienna is a city of palaces too. Schönbrunn, built to rival Versailles, possesses gardens that must be seen to be believed. The Hofburg is a complex of buildings, filled with history and art. And the Belvedere Palace, living up to its name, offers a superb view of Vienna looking towards the famous Vienna Woods; it is admittedly one of the finest baroque palaces in the world. You

will also easily see why Vienna claims the finest
and most considerable parks of any city in Europe.

SALZBURG

Rivaling Vienna as a tourist city is Salzburg,
perhaps known best as Mozart's town. Visually,
Salzburg enjoys the type of three-dimensional interest that one finds so often in European cities
(which were often built on or around citadels, for
very good reason). Dominating the town is the
Hohensalzburg fortress, which will remind you of
Edinburgh's great castle. Especially at night it is
a sight to behold, floodlit like the town's other
historic buildings. Substantially built in 1097, it
has been enlarged, notably by the Georgskirche,
at various times in Salzburg's long history.

The cathedral, too, has the sort of complex
history one would expect in this crossroads of
Europe. St. Virgil built the first structure, back
in 774. In 1181 it became a great Romanesque
five-aisled basilica. Then, early in the seventeenth
century it was rebuilt in "modern"—that is early
baroque—style, with a capacity of 10,500. St.
Peter's abbey church is even older, having been
founded by St. Rupert c. 969. The saint is buried
there, as is Michael Haydn, brother of the more
famous composer Joseph. The cemetery contains
interesting shrines and fantastic ancient Christian
catacombs.

The house of Mozart and the room in which he
was born will be visited by music-lovers. In the
house is a museum and collection of precious

manuscripts. There is, too, a Mozart square and the famous Mozarteum. The Salzburg Festival is, of course, deservedly world famous. But even before Mozart, Salzburg boasted of being "the Rome of the German world." It now claims to be "the heart of the heart of Europe." When you are there you will find it hard to disagree.

INNSBRUCK

Innsbruck is Austria's third tourist attraction, and as the capital of the Tyrol is one of the most picturesque spots in picturesque Austria. It is an ancient university town, parts of which date back to Roman times. Indeed, the Premonstratensian monastery of Wilten is on the site of Roman Valdilena. Among the churches in Innsbruck, most impressive is the sixteenth-century Hofkirche, unusual in being dominated by the monument of a Christian emperor, Maximilian, who is not buried there. Leading artists and sculptors (Dürer was one of them) collaborated in this immense work. But you will find it hard to resist taking tours out of Innsbruck—cable car rides especially. There is the Grossglockner Road trip, as well as several into Italy, to Bavaria (Oberammergau is not far), and throughout the Tyrol.

OTHER PLACES OF INTEREST

Even these treasures do not exhaust Austria. There is Linz (celebrated in one of Mozart's symphonies); there is Lower Austria with its five

hundred abbeys and castles; Carinthia, indescribably rich in castles and other architectural attractions, such as the venerable Romanesque cathedral
of Gurk and the ancient shrine of Maria Saal. So
immense is the variety that you will be hard put
to have a favorite. Between Vienna and Carinthia
is the ancient province of Styria, with its delightful
capital, Graz. The university, Johanneum museum
and stately cathedral—once the Jesuit church, until the Society's suppression in 1773—make Graz
attractive to visitors. Also in Styria, high and inaccessible, is one of Central Europe's most famous
pilgrimage centers, Mariazell, dedicated to Mary
the Great Mother of Austria.

SWITZERLAND

Since Switzerland's main industry is tourism and the country entertains several times its own population in tourists every year, just about everything you can expect does happen to the tourist. It is, of course, always the proper thing to downgrade Switzerland as "bourgeois," a nation of innkeepers, and the like; and the famous boutade in "The Third Man" about Italy producing Michelangelo, while Switzerland produced only the cuckoo-clock, is heard on all sides, at least in certain circles.

It seems that someone forgot about Le Corbusier, Klee, and Ansermet. Still, the tourist business thrives, as many thousands swarm over the Alps annually. One reason Americans like Switzerland is that they can have all the comforts of home, while enjoying just enough of the exotic. But there is more to be seen than Alps and cuckoo-clocks.

ZURICH

Although Berne lays claim to the title, there is really no capital of Switzerland in the sense that Paris is the capital of France or London of England. The greatest city is Zurich, a center of contemporary architecture, industry and modern art. The Kunsthaus ("Art Museum") has its ancient

masters, but is especially interesting for its four-
teen Cézannes (including several of those that
are most commonly reproduced), thirteen Degas,
and a great deal besides. The earliest inhabitants
of Zurich were lake dwellers (the city's name
derives from a Celtic word for "water"). In the
course of a long history a number of famous people lived and worked here—Zwingli, Pestalozzi,
Wagner, Jung. At the Reformation the cathedral,
an impressive Romanesque and Gothic building,
was austerely whitewashed within.

EINSIEDELN

From the historical and religious point of view,
however, nearby Einsiedeln has deeper roots.
"Einsiedeln" means "hermitage," much as "Mün-
chen" ("Munich") means "monks," and tells its
own history. The statue of the "Black Virgin"
(there are many such, but this and the one at
Montserrat are perhaps most famous) is one of
the main pilgrimage spots in Europe. The first
hermit here, St. Meinrad, arrived here about 828
with the statue. Although the present Benedictine
monastery building is not exceptional, it is the
sixth or seventh building on the spot. Throughout
the Middle Ages, Einsiedeln was a great spiritual
and cultural bastion of the Christian world. It is
one of the few monasteries to have been allowed
to exist continuously from Carolingian times to
ours. Just two miles to the south is a convent of

Benedictine nuns who offer "eternal" prayer in relays.

ST. GALL

Another of the great Swiss abbeys that have meant much to Christian civilization is not far to the east, St. Gall, the highest large town in Switzerland and one of the highest in Europe. St. Gall was an Irish missionary who came to this area around 614. The abbey itself developed under St. Othmar, and it is to the monks of St. Gall's abbey that we owe the preservation of many of the most valuable manuscripts of ancient learning. The town grew up beneath the abbey, to gain protection from Magyars and Saracens. Even today the Abbey library, one of the oldest in Europe, contains any number of treasures. The former abbey church is now the cathedral. Both, but especially the library, are so overpowering that you will feel you have never seen rococo till now.

LUCERNE

Toward the center of Switzerland is Lucerne, a city of delightful contrasts, with medieval, Renaissance and very contemporary buildings. There are two fourteenth-century wooden bridges, with paintings on their walls. The cathedral, which contains some fine craftsmanship, will please you with the liveliness shown by the faithful participating in Mass. The trip up Mount Pilatus is stunning, offering incredibly impressive views of the lake, city and surroundings.

BASEL

To the north and east lies Switzerland's second largest city, Basel, much like Bavaria in spirit and gaiety. Originally a Celtic settlement, we find it called Basilia by the Romans. In Church history, Basel was significant as the meeting place of an important and complicated Church Council (1431-1449). The illustrious Christian humanist of the period, Aeneas Sylvius, who had been present at the Council, later became Pope Pius II and founded the University of Basel. Another celebrated humanist, Erasmus, at one time lived and finally died here; his grave is within the splendid cathedral. Among other distinguished scholars associated with Basel were Vesalius, and in modern times Nietzsche and the historian Burckhardt. The Kunstmuseum ("Art Museum") possesses an exceptional selection of Holbein the Younger, who lived in Basel, and some valuable work of Gruenewald and Cranach, together with that of many moderns such as Kandinsky, Klee, Chagall, Picasso, Braque and Dali. One of Europe's very fine museums.

GENEVA

To the south and west, in the French-speaking region lies Geneva, beautifully situated on its famed lake. Nevertheless, Geneva manages to keep something of a dour aspect, as befits its renowned citizen, John Calvin, who once ruled here with a stern hand. Calvin's temperamental opposite, Jean-Jacques Rousseau, was born here, at No. 40 of the Grande Rue. Just north of the city, at Ferney-Voltaire, is the former house of Voltaire. In Geneva, the famed buildings are St. Peter's cathedral, the Reformation Memorial, and the rather unimaginative Palace of the League of Nations. The amiable St. Francis de Sales, bishop of Geneva, and one of the great lights of Church history, lived in nearby Annecy. His grave is there.

OTHER CITIES, OTHER CANTONS

Lausanne, an hour's drive northeast of Geneva along the lake, possesses an interesting history from Roman days to the present. There Gibbon and Voltaire became friends, and there Gibbon finished his *Decline and Fall of the Roman Empire.* There too, Swiss Protestantism remained so vigorous that Catholic church bells were not allowed until very recently. (I happened to be in town for the first ringing since the Reformation.) Farther along the lake shore you will find Montreux, a good place to take a mountain railroad up to some magnificent Alpine scenery. And, about three miles beyond, stands the famous Château de Chillon, right on the lake.

More interesting and picturesque is the capital of the neighboring canton, **Fribourg,** founded by

Berchthold, nephew of the founder of Freiburg-im-Breisgau (with which it is often confused by the unknowing). This area remained Catholic (the bishop of Fribourg is also bishop of Geneva and Lausanne). The Catholic University, though young (1889), is already renowned, not least for its superb modern architecture. The college of Saint-Michel, conducted by the Jesuits from 1585 almost without interruption to 1848, was founded by St. Peter Canisius, who is buried in the adjoining church. Since 1848, of course, Jesuits have not been allowed to remain in Switzerland. The cathedral of St. Nicholas is largely late Gothic. Nearby Berne, capital of the Confederation, is a quaint town, perhaps the most medieval-looking of the larger towns of Switzerland.

The **Ticino,** the only Italian-speaking canton, will make you feel you are already in Italy. The lakeside cities, Lugano and Locarno, are on lakes that continue into that land of sunshine. The Franciscan church of Santa Maria degli Angeli in Lugano, has some excellent frescoes by Luini, and San Lorenzo, the cathedral, is a noteworthy example of Renaissance art. The Villa Favorita contains an extraordinary art gallery that should not be missed. Locarno, on Lake Maggiore, is beautifully situated, and is dominated by a pilgrimage site, the Franciscan church of Madonna del Sasso, from which the view of the lake is breath-taking.

ITALY

Take at random ten visitors to Western Europe. Ask them to name their choices among countries they found most revealing, most stimulating, most moving—in a word, most interesting. There is no sure way to anticipate what country will come second; quite easily, in fact, it could be any one of those we have just seen in retrospect or anticipation, even one of the smallest. But the likelihood is that nine out of ten would add something like: "But, of course, Italy comes first."

And this is not just if your visitor happens to be a Catholic. To the North European, Italy is the incarnation of sunshine and the joy of living. Goethe nostalgically asks: "Kennst du das Land, wo die Zitronen blühn?" ("Do you know the land where the lemon trees bloom?") Yet even to the visitor from sun-drenched Spain or the French Midi, Italy is something special, both visually and in depth of meaning.

Nowhere do we meet such ranging contrasts of utter modernity and classic antiquity. Take the skyline of Milan, for example, or the Rome Railway Station, or generally the work of Pier Luigi Nervi, as well as Fellini's films or the music of Dallapiccola, Maderna, Berio or Nono; and juxtapose them with St. Peter's and Palestrina, or Venice's San Marco and Vivaldi.

On one of our European pilgrimages I recall a student, stirred by the Pantheon, who asked: "Why can't we build anything as wonderful as this today?" "Wait just a few minutes," was my rejoinder. When we drove over to see the new Palazzetto of Nervi, he quickly overcame the sense of inferiority. For, as Kidder Smith in his *The New Architecture of Europe* shows, "Italy is the only land of ancient splendor which has never died."

However, wondrous as much of Italy will prove in every way, whatever you do, be sure to allow your broadest stint of time and energy for Rome. Any other course will be poor economy.

If you arrive along the Riviera from France, the transition will have been prepared and may even prove imperceptible. On the other hand, if you leap abruptly through the new Mont Blanc tunnel or some other tunnel or pass from Switzerland, unless you have happily loitered in Lugano, you will be utterly dazzled by the change. You may even happen across someone idling in the sun (this actually was my experience when first arriving, through the Domodossola Pass, when Central and Northern Europe were still blanketed in winter)—strumming away and unconcernedly singing, in true *bel canto* style, "O Sole Mio." However, be not deceived by legend. The Italian, especially the Northern Italian, is not indolent; nor is he only a singer. The manifold cultural achievements of Italy are witness to the inexhaustible energy of its people.

GENOA

Driving in from France and Monaco, you will come to a great port city, with all the expected advantages and disadvantages. During the Middle Ages, Genoa was Venice's great commercial rival, and Pisa's too. You are in Italy now, remember, where civilization goes back even further than in the other ancient lands we have visited, and where centuries seem like decades. Genoa appears to be about as old as Rome, and was founded in the same eighth century B.C.

In the cathedral of San Lorenzo, begun by St. Lawrence himself, you will find a pleasant blend of Romanesque, Gothic and Renaissance—each period of its construction belonging to the style then contemporary. Among other famous Genoans are, of course, Columbus, Andrea Doria and the prodigious violinist Paganini; and their homes and monuments adorn the city, together with opulent palaces and some four hundred churches. Strange as it may sound, the Campo Santo, or cemetery, outside the city is among the most curiously fascinating spots to visit.

TURIN

North of Genoa is the region called Piedmont ("Foot of the Mountain"), a land of stupendous natural beauty, with a thoroughly industrialized capital, Turin. You will quickly find the Piazza San

Carlo, handsomely proportioned and well worth a leisurely visit. However, the white marble cathedral of San Giovanni, an imposing structure, has made Turin world famous largely because of its unique treasure, the Holy Shroud.

Volumes and volumes have been written for and against the genuineness of this relic. And no wonder. For if it is genuine,* it is uniquely precious, affording us the authentic image of Our Lord in a sort of photographic negative. Unfortunately, you will not be able to see the relic itself. It is a very ancient piece of cloth, which, being vulnerable to damage, is rarely exposed for photography and study. But you may see the silver casket in which it is preserved.

Turin glories in many saints, among them two great modern social apostles: the affable Don Bosco, helper of boys and founder of the Salesians, and Joseph Cottolengo, founder of the Piccola Casa ("Little House" of Divine Providence) for the poor and destitute.

It is an ancient royal seat as well. From Turin the House of Savoy once ruled Sardinia and subsequently all of Italy.

---

* I have attempted to read and assess the literature on the subject and have summed up what I believe a reasonable opinion, in the *Catholic Biblical Quarterly* Vol. 7, pp. 144-164. Father Walter Abbott, S.J. is of the same opinion, and has reviewed the subject in the *Catholic Encyclopedia* (*Supplement,* s.v. "Shroud, Holy"). We both believe that the Shroud is genuine, and we independently came to this opinion with some reluctance, after being much inclined to the other side.

MILAN

Milan, Rome's rival in population and as a cultural center, as well for a time the capital of the Western Empire, is easily the leading city of Italy in matters industrial and commercial. Opera enthusiasts, too, think of it as a capital, for it is the home of what may be the world's most distinguished opera house, La Scala. Lovers of art remember that it is the home of the West's most celebrated painting, Leonardo da Vinci's "Last Supper." But one should not overlook the Brera museum, a particularly representative collection of art. My favorite painting here is Piero della Francesca's "Madonna and Child Surrounded by Saints."

If your interest lies more in architecture, Milan will provide an exciting and immense variety of new work and three of the world's most valued older buildings: San Lorenzo, a venerable fourth-century church, in which the San Aquilino chapel is adorned with coruscating ancient mosaics; Sant'Ambrogio ("Saint Ambrose"), often studied as the perfect example of Italian Romanesque architecture; and the gigantic Duomo ("cathedral"), Christendom's fourth largest church, with its 135 marble spires and 2,245 marble statues.

The Duomo may be the largest Gothic cathedral in Europe, depending on your scale of measurement, but it is hardly one of the most perfect. However imperfect architecturally, and even without the spire that was intended as its crown, it is so staggering in its immensity that you tend to forget the neat rules of Gothic. (Further, it might be a useful idea to forget them for all of Italy; Italian Gothic is in a different category from other Gothic.) In the crypt of Duomo you will visit the grave of St. Charles Borromeo, one of the great reformers of the Church in the sixteenth century. But unless you feel able to tolerate peering at a skull and bony fingers amid gilded vestments, I suggest that you not ask to have the shrine opened. Attendants are only too eager to oblige for the expected gratuity.

Do visit the roof of the Duomo for a splendid panorama of the city, its striking new skyline, the green plains of Lombardy and the distant Alps. Formerly a city ordinance forbade building higher than the top of the highest spire and its beloved statue of Our Lady, the "Madonina." But apparently no ordinances restrict the use of the roof for picknicking and as a lovers' lane.

Milan is rich in history. Christians associate it with the spot at which Constantine proclaimed the so-called "Edict of Milan" (in 313), which freed them from persecution. St. Ambrose, one of the most influential Fathers of the Church, was bishop here, and here he baptized St. Augustine, greatest of them all. It was St. Ambrose, too, who inaugurated sacred music in the Western Church and left the tradition of the Ambrosian or Milanese rite— a Latin rite somewhat different from the Roman, as you will find when you attend Mass in Milan.

THE ENVIRONS

Within the vicinity of Milan are the lovely lakes of the North, which you may have seen from the Swiss side. The towns along the lakes seem the happiest of marriages between natural charm and appropriate human building. Mantua, home of the Gonzaga family and its most illustrious member, St. Aloysius, patron of youth, is nearby. Just outside Mantua, Virgil was born. The fact is commemorated in his alleged epitaph: *Mantua me genuit* . . . ("Mantua gave me birth"). Brescia, famed for St. Angela Merici, foundress of the Ursulines, is also quite an "art city," much like its neighbor, Bergamo. The Bergamo region has recently achieved further fame as the home of Pope John XXIII.

VERONA

You are now not far from Verona, known over the centuries for Catullus, the "Two Gentlemen" and Romeo and Juliet. Today you may attend superlative performances of opera in the old Roman arena—one of the largest and best preserved of Roman buildings—which accommodates twenty-five thousand spectators. The church of Sant'Anastasia is a very representative model of Italian Gothic, just as San Zeno Maggiore is one of the finest Romanesque-Lombard, with its harmoniously proportioned campanile. In the crypt

there you will find the tomb of St. Zeno, while on
the high altar is a triptych, one of Mantegna's
masterworks. A number of superb buildings sur-
round the Piazza dei Signori, as well as the impressive tomb of the Scaliger family, who long
ruled over Verona.

To the east is **Vicenza,** the city of Palladio,
whose architecture has probably exerted the widest
influence on American public-building styles, as
his basilica, Teatro Olimpico and especially the
Villa Rotonda (which is outside the city), will
clearly illustrate.

PADUA

Famous the world over, except in Portugal, as
the city of St. Anthony, beloved friend of the poor,
Padua has much to attract your interest. St. Anthony's basilica-tomb is, as you would expect,
venerated as a great shrine. Near it is one of the
finest equestrian statues in the world, Donatello's
"Gattamelata." Near, too, are ruins of a Roman
amphitheatre, reminding us that Padua is an old
Roman city. Livy was from here; an ancient critic
claimed to detect a trace of Paduan accent in the
historian's writing.

For the art historian Padua is a special treasure
trove, most of all for the Scrovegni Chapel (also
called the Arena Chapel), with the incomparable
frescoes of Giotto on its walls. Nowhere else will
you find represented in such profusion the works
of a man who, singlehanded, changed the current

of Western painting. The chapel, you will be reminded, narrowly escaped destruction during
World War II. When I was last there the bomb
crater, a few feet away, was a grim proof of the
precarious frailty of even our finest artistic monuments.

VENICE

Everything about Venice is so improbable that,
if it were not for photographs (and it is probably
the most photogenic city in Europe, as well as the
most frequently photographed, just as it was once
the most insistently painted), we should not trust
descriptions of it or our own memories. Even
when you are there, you find it hard to believe.
Then too, the enchanted atmosphere makes you
forget that this dream city was once a remote
refuge from barbarian incursions. Then later it
was a vast military and even militaristic power. It
is hard to conceive that it was the Venetians, not
the Moslems nor the ravages of time, that destroyed Athens' incomparable Parthenon; or that,
for long, Venice was the Wall Street of late medieval Europe. For more than a thousand years—
longer than either the Roman republic or empire
—Venice was a republic (only of sorts—surely in
no sense a democracy). And there it is now, and
there it has been, and there at least for some time
let us hope it will be, despite the gradual, irreversi-
ble sinking. At least, let us hope it will be there
long enough for you to visit it a few times.

Not even Rome seems to have more churches, and not even Rome can point to a more completely satisfying church than **San Marco,** opening on a piazza that is generally thought to be the handsomest in the world. San Marco is, beyond cavil, the heart and center of Venice. Built in 829-832 to enshrine the body of the evangelist St. Mark, which was brought from Alexandria in Egypt (where St. Mark had been bishop), it was rebuilt in the eleventh century. It is a superb example of Byzantine art, despite the later adornments.

As every ancient land or city, Venice has its tragic past. The fact that the four famous gilded horses on the façade of San Marco were plundered from Constantinople (1204) reminds us of the disastrous Fourth Crusade, which did irrevocable harm and helped consolidate Eastern distrust of the West. These statues are of antique Greek workmanship, dating back approximately to the period of Alexander the Great, but they are only a part of the cathedral's fine ornamentation. More meaningful is the vast mystery of Redemption, in golden mosaic, which one may study prayerfully and at leisure while walking around the sublime edifice. Everything connected with San Marco, even the dubious seventeenth-century mosaics in the façade, manages to add to the total splendor.

Within the cathedral, the placing of the two great organs opposite each other, has influenced the history of music. Always splendid and ornate, Venetian music has thus tended to use two en-

sembles, one near each organ, achieving a pe-
culiarly magnificent contrapuntal-antiphonal effect.

Next to San Marco is a symbol of Venice's past
worldly power and glory, the **Doges' Palace** (*doge*
is Venetian dialect for *duce* or "duke"; don't be
surprised if your classroom Italian doesn't quite
work in Venice, where "Venetian" is commonly
used in preference to "Florentine" or official
Italian). The palace, structurally of the fourteenth
and fifteenth centuries, is so fabulously ornate
as to make even Versailles seem somehow im-
poverished. While the columns of the ground
floor have sunk and lost some of their due proportions, the majestic building will thrill you, unless you are irreconcilably opposed to baroque.
Replete with Venetian painting—suitably as opulent as the city itself—the palace includes what
is reputed to be the largest oil painting in the
world, Tintoretto's "Paradise," the glowing visual
representation of Canto 30 from Dante's *Paradiso*.

Venice is the appropriate place to come to
know Tintoretto, Titian, Veronese, Giorgione, the
Bellinis, Carpaccio, Tiepolo and other Venetian
masters, who are often not worthily represented
even in large museums. For a concentrated view
of them, you will enjoy spending some time in
the **Accademia,** which has one of the world's
truly splendid collections. However, every church
and major building, and even individual palaces
along the Grand Canal, will reveal treasures of
that colorful, tumultuous school. The church of the
Frari, for example, contains two of Titian's master-

pieces, and near it is the Scuola San Rocco ("School of St. Roch"), where fifty-six of Tintoretto's most amazing works are gathered into a most stirring and revealing assembly. (Superlatives are thoroughly in order when one speaks of Venice.)

Across the Grand Canal from San Marco are two churches that will beckon you until you visit them. San Giorgio Maggiore ("St. George Major"), a masterpiece of the Palladium style and designed by the great architect himself, contains two of Tintoretto's most mature works, the "Last Supper" and the "Gathering of Manna," and offers a spectacular view of the city from an unusual vantage. Santa Maria della Salute ("St. Mary of Salvation"), in octagonal form and very baroque, seems to dominate the canal. Built as a votive offering to Our Lady, it is another of the churches that authorities on architecture like to include in their books. You will not wonder why.

After so much opulence, you may care to rest in a quiet enclave of Byzantium—the island of **Torcello,** with its fine octagonal church of Santa Fosca. There is a cathedral here too, founded in the seventh century and altered some during the Middle Ages; it is a gem of Byzantine architecture and still possesses elegant marble columns and mosaics. **Murano,** too, offers a choice of more Byzantine (in Santi Maria e Donato) or of Renaissance (San Pietro Martire).

After this contrast, returning to Venice, you find an indefinitely extended option of churches and

palaces, especially those like the Ca' d'Oro, along
the Grand Canal. For baroque gone mad, see
the enormous curtain that shrouds the pulpit in
the Jesuit church. You will be amused or outraged
when you touch it and discover that the curtain
is made of stone. But there are no limits to Venetian imaginativeness, especially as it ran wild in
the late baroque period.

Happily, not all art in Venice is old. Every two
years the Biennale exposition of modern art attracts the world's leading contemporary painters
and provides a welcome change for the viewer
after so much antique splendor. Every year, too,
in the Palazzo del Cinema, the international film
competition takes place. But opera and symphonic
music have always been at home in Venice. When
Petrucci began the widespread printing of music
here, in 1498, Venice became a world capital for
musicians, attracting Netherlanders, among them,
Adrian Willaert, and later Heinrich Schütz and
other Germans. The Gabrielis, Monteverdi, Cavalli
and Vivaldi, too, were among the galaxy of musical giants who lived and worked in Venice during
the Renaissance and baroque epochs.

RAVENNA

From Venice be sure to drive down to Ravenna,
which you will find to be one of Italy's invaluable
treasures. When Emperor Honorius, in A.D. 402,
decided that Ravenna would be a safer place
to live than Milan, he made it capital of the

Western Empire. Not even in Byzantium itself will you meet such incomparable Byzantine mosaics. Even after it was the last capital of the Western Empire, Ravenna became the favored city of the barbarian kings Odoacer and Theodoric, who continued to lavish adornment on the fair city.

Today Ravenna remains generally unspoiled, an artist's paradise, where time stands still. It is as much a city of the past as Venice; only, Ravenna's past is more remote. "Ravenna Felix" ("Ravenna the Fortunate") was its proud title in antiquity; today that device serves as the name of a journal of studies devoted exclusively to the city's artistic history.

Among Ravenna's proud buildings, we shall mention only a few. Ageless San Vitale, built under Emperor Justinian of Constantinople during the sixth century, may not greatly impress you from the exterior, despite its gently sloping, pyramidal massing. Nor will you be altogether happy when you first enter and see the tasteless eighteenth-century decoration. Move on in, however, and rejoice in the incredible glory and originality of the octagonal dome (closely imitated at Aachen in Charlemagne's chapel), and still more in the glory of the choir and apse mosaics. The panels of Justinian and his wife Theodora are considered the finest mosaic work of this first golden age of Byzantium.

Within the enclosure of San Vitale is another unique gem, the tomb of Empress Galla Placidia, sister of Honorius, benefactress and embellisher

of Ravenna. The building is shaped like a miniature, cruciform Byzantine church, with a dome at
the crossing. The interior illumined only through
alabaster windows presents an awesome atmosphere, coupled with the thrill of every shade of
blue. Agnes Carr Vaughan's novel, *Bury Me in
Ravenna,* recaptures much of the mood of the
building and period.

Since the Church in Ravenna is ancient, it enjoys certain local immunities and liturgical ec-
centricities. You will thus be interested in the cathedral itself, especially if you are lucky enough
to witness a procession of the cathedral canons,
like bishops bedecked with mitres. Next to the
cathedral is another Byzantine glory, the Ortho-
dox Baptistry, thoroughly adorned with mosaics
and marvels of every hue. The Arians' Baptistry,
Theodoric's creation, rivals it in majesty. Behind
the cathedral, in the museum, you will find a number of important objects of art, including more mosaics and the ivory sixth-century pulpit of Max-
imian.

The church of San Francesco, with its sarcopha-
gus of St. Liberius serving as high altar and
twenty-two columns of Greek marble, has been
recently restored. Near it is the grave of Italy's
supreme poet, Dante, who died here (1321) in
exile from his native Florence, and whose remains
the people of Ravenna have jealously kept, in hiding when necessary. Another famous tomb is that
of King Theodoric, built in 526 by the king's
daughter. Historians of art disagree about its style:

some hold that it is a combination of the barbarian tradition of burial under a great stone, with Roman and Byzantine building techniques; others believe that the great monolith is not here a barbarian motif, but part of a classic tradition. In any case, it is monumental and a worthy reminder of the man who did much for Ravenna.

The two celebrated churches dedicated to Ravenna's hallowed martyr, Saint Apollinaris, are classic examples of basilica structure. Within the city is Sant'Apollinare Nuovo, with its inspiring procession of saints that are popularly venerated in North Italy. Portrayed in resplendent mosaics, they move majestically forward above the colonnade toward the altar. You will be reminded of the procession in sculpture that adorned the frieze of the Parthenon (now among the Elgin marbles in the British Museum). In Sant'Apollinare, however, the procession is statelier and more in keeping with our liturgical concepts; and it is contained within the holy place, not without, as at the Parthenon.

The other basilica, Sant'Apollinare in Classe is so called because it used to be at the harbor, the late Roman Portus Classis, the station for the empire's fleet in the North Adriatic before the shoreline of the Adriatic receded. Here the principal interest lies in the great apse mosaic, glowingly portraying Christ surrounded by symbols of the four evangelists, above, the twelve lambs representing the apostles. The short side trip is well worth your time.

BOLOGNA

In contrast to timeless Ravenna, Bologna is a bustling city of commerce and industry. Yet, here too, there are shrines to be visited, both sacred and artistic. The tomb of St. Dominic, in the church dedicated to him, is itself a fascinating structure. San Stefano is a curious composite of eight churches, of varying periods and styles. Among them, the church of Calvary contains the tomb of St. Petronius; that saint's own church, begun in 1390, is not yet completed. Its central portal, by della Quercia, contains excellent early Renaissance sculpture. The Palazzo Communale, the porticoed streets, the leaning towers, and a plethora of palaces and churches make Bologna interesting to the tourist. And there is, as you would expect, a rich museum.

FLORENCE

South and west of Bologna lies Tuscany, a land predestined for art. Florence, its capital, has become almost synonymous with the Renaissance and its great art center, Italy. The city's heart is, again as in Venice, the great Duomo, Santa Maria dei Fiore ("Saint Mary of the Flowers"). This giant structure, begun in 1296, was not completed until Brunelleschi's dome crowned it in 1434; in fact, the present façade is fairly modern. Unadorned and majestic, the interior may strike you as cold, since, though Gothic, it lacks the warmth given by stained glass. As you examine it closer, however, you will discover any number of artistic treasures. Of these, the most eminent is Michelangelo's last sculpture, "The Descent from the Cross," in which the sculptor portrays himself as Joseph of Arimathea holding the Body of Christ, with the Blessed Virgin and Mary Magdalene assisting. This is surely one of the foremost groups of statuary in the world.

Alongside the cathedral, Giotto's immense campanile is itself a treasury of sculpture and marble work, and across the piazza is the baptistry, a vast octagonal structure that goes back many centuries. Three famous doors are masterpieces of bas relief: Pisano did the south door (1330), portraying scenes from the life of St. John the Baptist, to whom the baptistry is fittingly dedicated; Ghiberti did the north door (1403-24), which portrays scenes from the life of Christ and the Evangelists; and later did the east door—the one which Michelangelo believed "worthy to be the Gates of Paradise."

CHURCHES AND MUSEUMS

Of Florence's numberless churches it will be difficult to make a choice. Santa Croce, the giant Franciscan church, is a sort of Italian Westminster Abbey, containing the burial places of many famous personages: Michelangelo, Rossini, Galileo, Machiavelli and others. A number of Giotto's most admired paintings are here too, but in a much-restored condition. Adjoining the church is the elegant Pazzi Chapel, by Brunelleschi, a masterwork of Renaissance art.

The monastery of San Marco, formerly a Dominican friary where Savonarola and St. Antoninus lived, is the best place in the world to contemplate Fra Angelico's unearthly work. Building, cloister, stairwell and many individual friars' rooms are adorned by him with some of the most gracious and inspired painting in all Europe. Just opposite the staircase, for example, is Blessed Angelico's serene "Annunciation," of which copies are found everywhere.

The church of San Lorenzo, started by Brunelleschi, contains two magnificent sacristies: the older, by Brunelleschi himself, with works of Donatello, Lippo Lippi and Verrocchio; the newer, by Michelangelo, with the famous tombs and statues of Day, Night, Dawn and Twilight, together with his "Madonna and Child."

Santa Maria Novella, too, is a treasure of sacred art, with superb paintings by Masaccio (including his "Trinity," in its use of perspective one of the most revolutionary works in the history of painting) and Ghirlandaio, as well as the fine cloisters and works by Uccello. Masaccio is especially well represented in the church of the Carmine, where you will find paintings that helped determine the course of Western art.

High above Florence is the Romanesque church of San Miniato al Monte, one of the architectural masterpieces of the Middle Ages. While it is in-comparably rich in mosaic and painting, you may remember it best for the stunning view of the city. Somewhat below, the Piazzale Michelangelo of-fers another extraordinary vista of the city, the Arno and its famed Ponte Vecchio, and the distant summits of the Apennines.

The only view to rival or possibly surpass these is from the other side—Fiesole, the loveliest spot in the entire area. There you will enjoy the ancient Roman theater in its magnificent lofty setting, and the church of San Domenico, where you will be able to see other works of Blessed Fra Angelico. Be sure, too, to see Florence from Fiesole, prefer-ably at twilight, and take the ride down the moun-tain as darkness sets in.

Florence's museums are also inexhaustible and proverbial. The Accademia is especially valuable for its Michelangelo statues, notably the "David" and "The Captives." The Bargello is celebrated for other Florentine sculpture, including works of Donatello, Pollaiuolo and Verrocchio. The Pitti Palace includes several of Raphael's best known paintings, among them the "Grandduke Ma-donna," and a great quantity of Titians. To the rear lie the Boboli Gardens, where you may wish to attend a concert. I particularly remember Puc-cini's *Turandot* splendidly performed there.

But for Florentine painting taken as a whole, the pre-eminent museum is the Uffizi Palace. There, among hundreds of works familiar from textbooks, you find Botticelli's "Spring" and his

"Birth of Venus"; Leonardo da Vinci's "Adoration of the Magi"; Michelangelo's "Holy Family"; Raphael's "Leo X" and his "Madonna of the Goldfinch"; as well as Fra Angelico's "Coronation of the Blessed Virgin" and the astonishing "Portinari Altarpiece." You will not find it easy to tear yourself away from Florence.

Be sure to stop in **Pisa** at least long enough to see and climb the leaning tower and to visit the cathedral and baptistry, dazzling white against the piercing blue of Tuscany's sky. And Lucca, with its magnificent cathedral, as well as **Arezzo,** an ancient Etruscan town, should be seen. Arezzo has had a long history, with a phenomenal array of martyrs. It is also known as the birthplace of Petrarch and of Guido d'Arezzo, one of the most significant names in the history of music.

SIENA

Beyond question, Siena is one of the most enthralling spots in all of Italy, and, after Florence, the most important town in Tuscany. It is another of those uncanny places where time seems to have stopped. Still living in the Middle Ages, Siena may boast of a remarkable, shell-shaped Piazza del Campo, on which is the Gothic Palazzo Pubblico ("Town Hall") filled with representative paintings of the great Sienese school—Martini, Duccio and others. The cathedral, too, is Gothic, but with the peculiar ornateness expected in Italian churches. Its floor is strikingly inlaid in marble, and a sturdy octagonal opening dominates the crossing. Niccola Pisano, the father of Renaissance sculpture, did the pulpit.

Siena's Pinacoteca is, appropriately, a treasury of Sienese painting, notably of Duccio and his school. But Siena's greatest citizen—indeed, one of the most influential women in all world history —is St. Catherine. She it was who persuaded Pope Gregory XI to return to Rome from Avignon, thereby helping to preserve the Church from further disastrous schism. Her relics are venerated in the church of San Domenico. You will want to visit her house, too, but I suggest not at the siesta hour. I have an unpleasant recollection of the custodian's temper at that sacrosanct time.

Near Siena is the monastery of Monte Oliveto, where a special group of Benedictines called "Olivetans" were established.

UMBRIA

The region of Umbria is just about midway between Florence and Rome. Following your visit to Arezzo, you will go by Lake Trasimeno, where Hannibal won a battle over the Romans (217 B.C.) that almost changed the course of history. Then comes **Perugia,** a town of singular grace and interest. Besides a fine cathedral, Perugia possesses a variety of picturesque and venerable churches famed for their saints and their art. In the Palazzo Communale is a gallery that specializes in Umbrian painting, with masterworks of Perugino and his school.

Not far away is Spoleto, one of the typically haunting hill towns of Umbria, which has recently soared into world popularity thanks to Menotti's annual Festival of Two Worlds. And be sure to allow time for Orvieto and its cathedral—one of the most ornate but harmonious in Italy, with marble stripes much like those of Florence's cathedral. It encloses some impressive paintings by Fra Angelico with other artists.

ASSISI

However, Umbria's most lovely town, and, apart from Rome itself, perhaps the most beloved shrine in all Italy, is Assisi. The sheer charm of the hill town, its protean views, as well as what man has done to add humanity to nature, all contrive to make Assisi truly worthy of its gracious saint, or rather, saints. Be sure to assist at the Holy Sacrifice near the very spot where St. Francis is buried, allowing yourself time to meditate and absorb some of his spirit. His basilica, with its superimposed churches, is enormously impressive and has been further enhanced by Cimabue, Giotto and pupils of Giotto.

Below the town is the holy place where St. Francis died, Santa Maria degli Angeli ("Saint Mary of the Angels"), with its privileged Porziuncula chapel. And high above, linking heaven and earth, is the Eremo degli Carceri ("Hermitage of the Prisons") where the Saint loved to pray; here, all nature seems to join him in a canticle of creation.

Two other Franciscan sites are especially sacred here: the oratory of San Damiano, where Our Crucified Lord spoke to St. Francis, where the saint composed "The Canticle of Brother Sun," and where he gathered St. Clare and her companions; and the church of Santa Chiara ("St. Clare"), where her holy body reposes. There is much besides to see in Assisi, all fragrant with the great spirit of St. Francis and St. Clare.

ROME

"And now what can I say of Rome, but that it is the first of cities, and that all I ever saw are but as dust (even dear Oxford inclusive), compared with its majesty and glory?" The words were written by that sensitive Oxonian, Newman, in a letter to his sister, Harriet. No more need be said in exhortation to the European visitor; to visit Europe without paying a pilgrimage to Rome is to miss the heart and soul of all.

Even today, culturally as well as religiously, all roads lead there. The great advantage of seeing Rome last is that you thus save yourself the disappointment of other sights, which cannot fail to be anti-climatic. Accordingly, if you are to see the South of Italy and Sicily—and I urge this as strongly as possible—you may do well to skip

Rome at this point, or at least hurry through it, and then come back to Rome for as long as you can afford.

For a good view of Rome as a whole, climb to some high spot like the dome of St. Peter's, or better still, to the Borghese Gardens or the Janiculum, where you can see St. Peter's. If Oxford is a city of towers (as Rome too was during the Middle Ages), Rome today is a city of domes, majestic domes, dozens of them, echoing the sublime theme of St. Peter's. In fact, if early in your visit you enter the Pantheon, you will discover the key to this proliferation of domes. Bramante's ambition, as he put it, was to "raise the dome of the Pantheon upon the vaults of Constantine's basilica." Emile Mâle, who enjoys good title to being the leading authority on sacred art, finds that Bramante's "tremendous dream has been realized. In St. Peter's, the antique world is brought to life again, and it was never so splendid." As Mâle points out, Rome is now basically a Renaissance and baroque city. There, best of all, we may learn what the Renaissance was. "It was," to quote Mâle again, "antiquity ennobled by the Christian Faith."

There can be little question that the spiritual and artistic hub of the Christian world is **St. Peter's.** By no means the most beautiful church in the world (whatever that may mean), it is easy to criticize when one is sitting back home in the comfort of an armchair. However, even when you visit it alone, you discover that it is assertive, almost overpowering; when you are there amid throngs of the faithful, and most of all when the Vicar of Christ is being carried toward the high altar, under which the Prince of the Apostles is buried, any thought of criticism seems frivolous indeed. Though the church of St. John Lateran, where the Popes first lived after the days of persecution, is technically Rome's cathedral, St. Peter's remains the shrine of shrines, a place where the faithful vociferously honor Christ by honoring his first vicar, beneath the altar, and his present one, visible here. Even Emerson, who had no religious reasons to venerate the great basilica, admitted: "It is an ornament of the earth."

You must make several visits to do justice to St. Peter's. The pilgrimage to the crypt, where St. Peter was buried, close to the place of his martyrdom, will bring you in spirit to those apostolic times. But St. Peter is only one of many popes to be buried there, and you will want to make many smaller pilgrimages to the shrines of his saintly successors, whose remains lie under side altars and elsewhere in the basilica: St. Gregory the Great, for instance, or St. Leo, or St. Pius X. You will surely buy a special guidebook to St. Peter's, if you are not to miss a great deal—touching objects like the Michelangelo "Pietà," and those pitiful tombs of the last Stuarts, the uncrowned monarchs James Francis Edward, Charles Edward, Henry, Cardinal of York.

Some of the more obvious thrills, of course, will come from the dome itself—seen from within or without—with its monumental inscription giving sense and focus to everything you see about you: "Thou art Peter, and upon this Rock I will build my Church, and I will give you the keys of heaven."

The Piazza San Pietro is a vast atrium or court-yard opening wide to receive you to the heart of Christendom. In keeping with the curving lines of the baroque style, architect Bernini made it neither square nor rigidly circular, but ovoid. Despite its immensity (it holds some five hundred thousand, though estimates do not concur), it is a conception of great subtlety and refinement, with its 284 enormous columns (it will take five of you, arms outstretched, fingertip to fingertip, to encompass a single column), in triple rows, its two expressive fountains, and a central, cross-crowned obelisk. The only thing really wrong with the ensemble was not Bernini's fault, much less Michelangelo's: the gorgeous façade, added by Maderno, is so vast that it obstructs the view of Michelangelo's dome from the piazza, where it should best be seen. However, here too, you will tend to agree with Henry James, who observed that what St. Peter's "lacks in beauty, it makes up in certainty."

Within the **Vatican** proper there is an unbelievable hoard of art to examine. Obviously, most important is the Sistine Chapel, with its superb paintings by Perugino, Botticelli and others. It is dominated by the awe-inspiring Michelangelo "Last Judgment" behind the altar, and the colossal ceiling frescoes dealing with Creation and

other great truths—the former done when Michelangelo was an old man, the latter in his youth.
As you have heard, it is hard to get a good view
of the chapel's paintings because of the throngs
that clutter up the place. The only remedy is to
arrive very early in the morning, and rush quickly
to the chapel, leaving everything else to a later
visit.

What I referred to as "everything else" includes
some of the sublimest art in Rome. In the nearby
apartments you will find Raphael's masterly *stanze*
("rooms"). In one of them are the "Disputà," in
which he sums up, in a vast catholic synthesis, all
values revealed in nature and supernature, and
the "School of Athens," which may be thought of
as the philosophical counterpart to the "Disputà."

The Vatican Picture Gallery too contains works
by many of the great masters and is a major museum; however, I feel that you may allot less time
here, since most of the masters represented may
be found even better represented elsewhere. However, you can hardly afford to miss the Raphael
"Transfiguration" (his last work) and "Coronation of the Blessed Virgin." In the Pio-Clementino
Museum, also in the Vatican, are two of antiquity's most familiar statues: the "Laocoön"
group and the "Apollo Belvedere." But, even
more important, within the Vatican Library you
will find an incredible treasury of manuscripts,
among them what is probably the most precious
book in the world, the *Codex Vaticanus* of the
Bible.

Rome's second jewel is the tomb and basilica of St. Paul—**St. Paul's-Outside-the-Walls.** While much of it was rebuilt following a calamitous fire in the last century, St. Paul's retains the authentic flavor of an ancient Roman basilica. The restoration was tastefully and accurately done, and in 1854 Pius IX reconsecrated the holy place (the same year in which he defined the dogma of the Immaculate Conception). In one of the chapels facing the transept—one not destroyed by the fire —St. Ignatius Loyola took his final vows. The stately Arch of Triumph, near the high altar, is covered by a fifth-century mosaic, and the five colonnades of granite contribute to one of the most impressive interior views in the world. The cloister, too, is very congenial, with its colorful medieval Cosmatesque mosaics.

OTHER CHURCHES

Two other churches are also called major basilicas: St. John Lateran, officially the Pope's cathedral, and Santa Maria Maggiore ("St. Mary Major"). While both have been considerably restored and added to, you will surely find them impressive, even if imperfectly satisfying. St. Mary Major contains the finest mosaics in Rome and some expertly done frescoes; its ceiling was adorned with the first gold brought back from America by Columbus.

The church of San Pietro in Vincoli ("St. Peter-in-Chains") claims great antiquity, but is best known for Michelangelo's great statue of Moses, the statue that the sculptor is said to have ordered to speak. Yet another ancient church is Santa Maria in Cosmedin, with its unique mosaic pavement and interesting architecture. And the basilica of San Clemente is fascinating for its triple structure: the top level is eleventh and twelfth century, erected over the older church built by Constantine, which in turn was constructed over what is believed to be the house of St. Clement, one of the earliest popes. At this lowest level, next to St. Clement's house, is a Mithraic temple. One wonders whether the small lane between them was ever bridged by some form of primitive interchurch dialogue.

The fifth-century church built over the house of SS. John and Paul (which goes back almost to the period of St. Clement's), is further honored by the remains of St. Paul of the Cross. The great founder of the Passionists is buried in a side chapel, where he is much venerated by the faithful.

Still more ancient, indeed the most ancient complete building in Rome is the Pantheon, which has been used as a church since Pope Boniface IV appropriately consecrated it, in 609, to Our Lady and All the Martyrs. Built under Agrippa in 27 B.C., it was given its present façade under Hadrian, about A.D. 130. Nowhere can the excellence of Roman building, particularly in the mastery of the dome, be better observed. There is, in fact, something absolute about the Pantheon.

No wonder that it has been used as a burial place for famous men, among them Raphael. (There is a classic story about the Pantheon that bears repeating. When a pope of the Barberini family allowed the bronze from the dome to be detached and used for the *baldacchino* over the high altar of St. Peter's, Roman wags uttered an epigram: "What the barbarians didn't do, the Barberini did" —*Quod non fecerunt barbari, fecerunt Barberini.*)

If not as old in time, even more venerable among holy places, where the pilgrim enters the presence of an incalculable army of martyrs and saints, undergirding as it were the Holy City itself —Rome's catacombs. Miles and miles around and under Rome they spread. But the most celebrated are those of St. Callixtus, St. Cecilia, St. Domitilla and St. Sebastian. While there has been an amount of imaginative exaggeration about the catacombs, including the extravagant term, "Church of the Catacombs," used to describe the early Church, they are nonetheless truly sacred; and what may be just as useful to the pilgrim, they *feel* sacred. Few experiences are more consoling than that of offering Mass where the saints, in such profusion, were buried after making their own supreme sacrifice.

If perhaps not as dramatically satisfying, the Mamertine Prison is at least equally venerable. It is found at the entrance of San Giuseppe dei Falegnami ("St. Joseph of the Carpenters"). At the lowest level, called San Pietro in Carcere ("St. Peter in Prison"), is the traditional spot where

St. Peter is thought to have been imprisoned before his crucifixion on Vatican Hill. Other notables, such as those famous enemies of Rome, Jugurtha and Vercingetorix, are also believed to have been imprisoned here.

The churches of St. Pudentiana and St. Praxedes also touch apostolic times, even if the present buildings date largely from the fourth or fifth centuries. That of St. Pudentiana is believed to be on the site of the house where St. Peter received hospitality.

"Hospitality" reminds me of another church in the vicinity, a church not mentioned in the guide books, and surely much less distinguished than the ancient shrines we have been mentioning. However, if you take a moment to visit the church of Madonna dei Monti ("Madonna of the Mountains") on Via dei Serpenti, you will encounter no tourists and few well-dressed pilgrims. For this is the refuge of the down-and-outers, who, like their patron, St. Benedict Joseph Labre, seem to feel more at home here than in God's more splendid houses. The saint literally lived here and is buried here, his spirit still giving comfort and a sense of holy brotherhood to the underprivileged. You will not soon forget your visit to this shrine.

Santa Croce ("Holy Cross"), built to house the relic which St. Helena, Constantine's mother, brought back from the Holy Land, has been considerably rebuilt, but is still impressive. You will be particularly fortunate if you can be here on Good Friday or other special feasts when the relic of the Holy Cross is exposed for the veneration of the faithful. And be sure to read Evelyn Waugh's masterly work *Helena,* before, during or after your pilgrimage here.

Among the important baroque churches of Rome, three are appropriately associated with saints of the Society of Jesus. In the Gesù we find the prototype of many churches of the Counter-Reformation. Built by Vignola and other architects, including two Jesuit lay brothers named Tristano, the Gesù houses the Society's principal shrines: the image of Our Lady of the Wayside, the altar above the grave of St. Ignatius Loyola, that enshrining the arm of St. Francis Xavier, and until recently, the tomb of St. Andrew Bobola (whose body was rather dramatically whisked out of Communist Russia in true cloak-and-dagger fashion).

The church of St. Ignatius is also world famous for its amazing visual perspective. The gigantic fresco in the dome, painted by Father Antonio Pozzo, showing St. Ignatius entering heaven, is one of the unique sights of Rome. Three treasured altars here enclose the remains of SS. Robert Bellarmine, Aloysius Gonzaga and John Berchmans. Totally different, and ever so much more pleasant to visit, is the charming little church where St. Stanislaus Kostka is buried. This fine structure, planned in his favorite elliptical form, is one of Bernini's masterpieces, and a place where the great architect loved to pray in his old age. St. Stanislaus' statue is, to my way of thinking, even

more deplorable than saints' statues are wont to
be. However, within the sacristy, hanging on the
wall, is the unique letter of one saint to another
about a third: St. Peter Canisius recommending
St. Stanislaus Kostka to St. Francis Borgia.

If you are involved in education—as teacher,
parent or student—you will want to make a quiet
pilgrimage to the shrine of the patron of all educa-
tors. On Via Aurelia, in the Mother House of the
Brothers of the Christian Schools, you will venerate the remains of St. John Baptist de la Salle,
buried under the side altar in the chapel. The Saint
was born in Rheims (where you may visit the very
house of his family) and died in Rouen, but his
body was transferred to Rome, the center of his
Institute, the largest order of men dedicated entirely to Christian education.

TREASURES OF AN EMPIRE

There are museums, too, in this vast museum-
city. That of the Capitoline, for example, contains
the famed statue—the "Dying Gaul," as well as
much other classic sculpture. The Borghese Gallery, situated handsomely in the gardens of the
same name, is rich in paintings, especially those
of Titian and Correggio. The Terme possesses the
textbook favorite statue, "The Discus Thrower,"
and other works that you will recognize. And the
gigantic Castel Sant'Angelo (Hadrian's Tomb) is
itself a museum and a rather formidable place to

visit; it is easy to recall scenes from Puccini's *La Tosca.*

The fuller truth about Rome, however, is much more than a matter of the past, however glorious that past was. Rome today is a vital, sophisticated, contemporary city, too, and has never ceased to be so—though there was a gruesome period of the early Middle Ages which is called "Iron" rather than "Golden." However, not everything in modern Rome is attractive (witness the lamentable Victor Emmanuel monument variously called "The Wedding Cake" or "The False Teeth"). But in Rome, perhaps more than anywhere, one is reminded how shallow and limited a mere tourist's viewpoint must inevitably be. For to the Romans of today, Rome is not principally a matter of history or even of shrines. It is home, today. And to everyone, today and tomorrow matter more than yesterday.

Yet to us, mere visitors, remain the countless relics of antiquity, both sacred and secular, and nowhere may we become as sharply aware of continuity and tradition as in Rome. A casual stroll, down Rome's ancient Via Sacra (reminiscent of Horace and his *Ibam forte Via Sacra* . . .); through one or other Forum; or up and down amid the labyrinthine Palatine Hill, with all its levels of ruined palaces; or through the maze of what was once called Nero's "Golden House"; or in and about the Coliseum (named after Nero's long-perished colossal statue—and a holy place despite vulgar commercialism); or through the various poignant triumphal arches, and the theaters and baths (those of Caracalla, for example, where you may be lucky enough to attend an opera); to the summit of the Capitoline; along Rome's graceful boulevards; to San Gregorio, now a Camaldolese monastery, where St. Gregory sent St. Augustine to convert England, and where you will hear the finest Gregorian chant in Rome; along the Via Flaminia up to the Milvian Bridge, where on October 28, 312, Constantine had his vision and defeated Maxentius; down the endless, history-laden Via Appia, lined with monumental tombs of Rome's great families; above the Spanish Steps to the Trinità, where *Mater Admirabilis* reigns so graciously, and to San Alfonso (on Via Merulana), where she reigns as Our Lady of Perpetual Help; over to Trastevere and the Isola Tiberina, possibly the most Roman part of Rome, and where the Brothers of St. John of God continue his godly work; past many unbelievable fountains, Trevi and others; through what were once called circuses, the ruins of temples and past pitiful half-standing columns—all this, and much besides, may occupy you meditatively and with a sense of the wonder and grandeur and transience of human things. There is irony in the Eternal City.

TIVOLI AND THE ALBAN HILL TOWNS

Rome is a solitary city, without suburbs in the ordinary sense. Its neighboring towns (once its enemies) have their own fascination. Tivoli, for example, has two exceptional attractions: the Villa d'Este gardens, with their symphonic fountains, among the finest in Europe; and the Emperor Hadrian's even less believable villa. Long before Hadrian, Tivoli (the Roman Tibur) had been a resort area, where Horace had his country house and his richer friends their elaborate villas. The Hadrian villa, as you will discover, is an enormous estate. Stewart Perowne, in his biography of Hadrian, describes it rather as "an Empire Exhibition, a whole Garden City, to recreate in miniature the regions of the empire which had most caught the fancy of their imperial inspector." The 750 acres included reproductions of the finest buildings of Greece and some of Egypt. Hadrian (like Horace) had enjoyed the lovely valley of Tempe in Thessaly; so he had a valley "built" to remind him of Tempe. Nothing was spared to create "the largest monument to the Good Life ever constructed." Hadrian, when he wanted solitude to philosophize, particularly enjoyed an island (to which only he had access), on an artificial lake. Today all you see are ruins of this fantastic project, but what you do see you are not likely to forget.

Visit the Rocca di Papa and the venerable abbey of **Grottaferrata,** founded by St. Nilus in 1004. In style it is Byzantine, a vivid reminder of the universality, not just the Latinity, of the Catholic Church. Back in Rome, near St. Mary Major, in the Russicum College, you will be reminded again, as you witness the magnificent Russian liturgy performed in all its dignity and mystery.

The Pope's summer residence, Castel Gandolfo, is just nearby, and so is Palestrina, a very ancient town, whose most celebrated citizen, Pierluigi, is commonly known simply as "Palestrina." And the old port of Rome, **Ostia,** is now well connected with the City by subway and superhighway. This is the town with recollections of St. Augustine, Father of the Church, and of his saintly mother, Monica. Amid antiquities here, one may sense the past even more completely than in Rome, where past and present overlap and commingle.

SUBIACO AND MONTE CASSINO

Another pair of saints that may be called pillars of Christendom are venerated near Rome, at one of Christendom's holiest spots. Not far from Tivoli, is Subiaco, the birthplace of Western monasticism, sacred to St. Benedict and his sister St. Scholastica. Here came the young patrician Benedict, aged seventeen, about the year 497, when Italy struggled for its life under the Ostrogoths, and just about the time that Ravenna rose to pre-eminence. Benedict had left his wealthy home near Spoleto to live for Christ as a poor solitary. From the disciples who gathered round him, he formed small monastic units. Later he moved to Monte Cassino, midway between Rome and Naples, where he wrote the Holy Rule that has been the way of life for many hundreds of thousands of holy Christian men and women. Monte Cassino has, of course, been destroyed many times—most recently by the Allies in World War II—but it always rises from its ruins.

St. Benedict modestly thought of his rule only as "a little rule for beginners." Avoiding the ascetical extravagances of Eastern and Irish monastic practice, he, like a good Roman, urged moderation, prudence and holy discretion, together with a family spirit that stressed stability. Over the centuries, a proliferation of monasteries made many oases of Christian life and civilized order in a world troubled and in general disarray. No words can overstate Benedict's role in the preservation and creation of everything that we value highest; there can be no question that St. Benedict is a father of Christendom, as well as of monasticism.

NAPLES

The superhighway now linking Rome to Naples makes it possible to drive in two hours from the Coliseum to Pompeii, both classic types of ancient ruins. Naples ("New City" it means literally in Greek) is among the most historic cities of Italy. The fact that its name is Greek reminds us that all of the south of Italy, as well as Sicily, were Greek before they were Roman, known as Magna Graecia ("Greater Greece"). Owing to the movement of history, especially the industrial revolution, which favored the north, Naples is no longer rich and powerful; indeed, it is one of the most wretched-looking cities of Western Europe. Yet, somehow, the natural beauty of its site, on one of the world's most superb bays, gives validity still to the old proverb, "See Naples and die." (I am aware that the proverb has more than one interpretation, but am content to follow the commoner one.)

The cathedral of Naples is (as one would expect from his worldwide reputation) named after Saint Januarius (**San Gennaro** in Italian). Here, twice a year, on schedule, takes place one of the most bizarre miracles authenticated by competent observers. (I personally have not been present to see the miracle, but have talked with scholarly, non-hysterical persons who have witnessed it at arm's length. No impartial student now questions the fact, even though all are bewildered by its symbolism.) The blood of St. Januarius, kept in a round vial, liquifies on the saint's feast, September 19, and on the first Saturday of May. At the same moment, in Pozzuoli, where the saint was martyred, ancient patches of blood are seen to become a bright red. The strangeness of this wonder, as well as its almost exact predictability, make it unique in the annals of hagiography.

Naples is replete with churches, and you will find the churches replete with devout people. However, it may require more than one's usual tolerance to approve the styles of devotion to be observed here. For in some of these churches, manifestations of piety that most of us would deem

odd, or at least peripheral, seem to enjoy the
ascendancy. Yet, I strongly suspect that a great
benefit of our pilgrimage to Naples' shrines and
churches may be an enlargement of our American
sense of the meaning of Catholicism. We, like
everybody else, all too easily tend to imagine ours
as *the* real Christianity. It could be that the incon-
ceivable miracle of St. Januarius, for all its weird-
ness, may do us spiritual good in a way quite other
than it does the Neapolitans.

The **National Museum** of Naples is of unique
value for the study of ancient art, especially that
of Magna Graecia. Among famous works here,
is the giant mosaic picturing the battle of Darius
of Persia and Alexander the Great. While there
are several fine paintings here too, the better
museum for these is the Capodimonte Palace, with
scores of Velázquez, El Greco, Breughel, and, of
course, any number of Italian artists. However,
no museums can replace visits to Herculaneum
and Pompeii, near Mount Vesuvius. In either
town, you will do well to buy a guidebook, keep
severely away from all other guides and do your
own exploring.

But Naples is more than a city of visual beauty.
Particularly in the eighteenth century it was a great
center of music. The two Scarlattis (father and
son) were Neapolitan, as was that prodigious
young genius, Pergolesi. Opera has always thrived
there, and even today, the San Carlo Opera is
world famous. In the popular field, every year the
Piedigrotta shrine of Our Lady is the site of a huge

competition, in which the best songs of the season are played and awards given in accord with popular acclamation and the judgment of a jury.

THE ENVIRONS

Naples' vicinity is a source of endless fascination. There are spots like Virgil's tomb (though no scholar believes he is buried there), with its wonderful inscriptions, tributes from other Italian poets down the centuries. Pozzuoli's Roman amphitheater is worth seeing, too, as is Lake Averno, where, according to the *Aeneid,* Aeneas descended into the underworld. Near the lake is the grotto of the Sibyl of Cuma.

The island of **Capri** is as beautiful as the stories about it. Though overrun by tourists of the cruder type, it is still bewitching, the Blue Grotto even more than the rest of the island. The **Amalfi Drive,** too, is another of the wonders of the world. I suggest that you take it twice, in both directions. At Amalfi, in the cathedral, the body of St. Andrew the Apostle is venerated. Sorrento, suffering like Capri from overpublicity, is usually overcrowded, but offers enchanting views of the Bay of Naples, Capri, Ischia and the surrounding area.

Salerno, situated on its own colorful gulf, is a picturesque town, where, during the Middle Ages, there thrived a school of medicine that has exerted an enormous influence on the history of ideas. And do, by all means, take the cable ride of Castellamara and climb Mount Faito for the most beautiful view in all the area. And I urge you not to be one of those tourists too much in a hurry to visit **Paestum,** with perhaps the finest assembly of Greek temples to be found anywhere. They are most impressive, these ancient Doric edifices, in their deserted grandeur.

SICILY

The South, for all its destitution, deserves a trip to itself. And Sicily, ancestral home of millions of Americans, has been—longer than any spot in the Western world—one of the richest of cultural centers. In its long, eventful history, it has been Greek (Archimedes lived there, for example, and Plato, and any number of other celebrated pioneers of civilization); Carthaginian, until Rome won it as her first province, following a bloody Punic War; Arab; Norman; and, more or less, Italian.

Monreale's cathedral contains some six thousand square yards of the world's richest mosaics. Cefalù, another ancient Greek city, points to its stupendous Norman cathedral. Palermo is a microcosm of many civilizations, with monuments of them all. And Syracuse keeps, even today, much of its fabled charm. It has been asserted that no other city is so "laden with history." In his day, Cicero described Syracuse as "the greatest of Greek cities and one of the most beautiful in the world." When he said this, Athens and Ephesus and Alexandria were still gloriously standing.

The opposite shores of the Straits of Messina,

the Scylla and Charybdis of classic legend, are now
soon to be linked by a one hundred and twenty
million dollar bridge. Thus, Sicily may begin to
lose some of its isolation and autonomy. Oil has
been discovered there and methane in Lucania,
the poorest part of Italy. This entire destitute area
may thus be destined to a revival of prosperity.
Doubtless the Sicilians and other southern Italians
would appreciate this. For it is impossible to live
on past glory alone.

*   *   *

And now, before returning to America, do go
back to Rome, putting your whole pilgrimage into
fullest and sharpest perspective. True, there are
older cities, and perhaps lovelier ones, and others
that bind with a charm all their own. But no other
is so lastingly full.

Gibbon and smaller men, lacking the vision of
faith, have seen Rome as something declining or
fallen. Constrasting Rome's ancient broken columns, as I walked among them yesterday, with
today's stream of Vatican Council Fathers pour-
ing out of St. Peter's basilica—and especially with
Peter's newest successor, so aged, yet so vigorous
—I found it not hard to see Providence eternally
present here.

Rome, December 8, 1962

GLOSSARY

apse. A domed or vaulted projection at the end of an aisle or choir, often a recess back of the altar in a basilica or church; usually semicircular or rounded.

arabesque. A surface decoration; in Arabian style, made of flowing scrolls or patterns of flowers or leaves, fancifully arranged.

baldacchino. A canopy commonly built over an altar.

baroque. The style (prominent from about 1600-1750) commonly associated with the Counter Reformation. Characterized by dramatic, sometimes theatrical, traits; flowing lines; suggestion of movement and organic relationships between various parts of building.

basilica. Originally a Roman public building, rectangular in plan, with a wide central nave, flanked by aisles and separated from it by columns; adopted by Christians as an early church style.

Byzantine. The art of Byzantium (Constantinople) and the Eastern Roman Empire. Characterized by lavish use of mosaic and splendor of conception; the dome is often featured in this style.

campanile. A bell tower related to a church, sometimes attached to the church, sometimes near it.

Carolingian. Pertaining to Charlemagne and his empire. The Carolingian Renaissance is characterized largely by massive monastic building and illuminated manuscripts.

chevet. Apse, choir, chapels radiating from the back or "eastern" end of the church.

choir. The area reserved for the choir in front of the altar; usually back (or "east") of the transept.

fresco. Painting on freshly-spread plaster.

Gothic. The style of art common especially in Northern Europe from the twelfth century to the Renaissance. In architecture it is generally characterized by the use of pointed arches; ribbed vaulting; flying buttresses; an emphasis on light. In general, later Gothic tends to be more ornamental (called "flamboyant" in France, "perpendicular" in England).

lantern. Opening on top of a dome or roof, principally to admit light.

Lombard. The Romanesque style of Northern Italy.

Manueline. The fanciful, highly ornamented style associated with Portuguese late Gothic and baroque. It often includes maritime and exotic motifs, suggestive of Portugal's vast exploits on the sea.

mosaic. Designs of images made out of small pieces of stone or glass (called tesserae) set in fine cement plaster.

narthex. Porch forming vestibule of a church; usually contains columns.

nave. The main body of a church.

Palladian. The neo-classic style of architecture associated with Andrea Palladio (1518-1580).

plateresque. The jewel-like style of Spanish architecture and decoration of the sixteenth century (from *platero* or "silversmith").

Renaissance. Any revival or quickening in human endeavor. Usually applied, in the arts, to the fifteenth century (a century earlier in Italy), influenced by classical literature, architecture and sculpture. Characterized by a sense of repose, human dimensions, the use of Greco-Roman columns and other classical motifs.

reredos. An ornamental screen back of the altar or on it. Sometimes identified with "retable," the frame enclosing painted or carved panels in back of the altar.

rococo. The delicate, slender, vivacious style common in the eighteenth century, often regarded as an extension of the baroque. Highly ornamental.

Romanesque. The style of art, based on Roman, common in Western Europe after Charlemagne, especially in the eleventh and twelfth centuries. Characterized in architecture by semicircular arches, barrel vaulting, a general feeling of mass (often combined with great height), and, especially toward the end of the period, the use of stained glass. Usually called "Norman" in England.

transept. In a cross-shaped church, the parts that are built at right angles to the main part or nave. English Gothic cathedrals sometimes have two sets of transepts. The area where nave and transepts meet is called "the crossing."

vaulting. Arched roofing in stone or brick (or concrete). "Barrel" vaults are shaped like a half-barrel. "Ribbed" vaults have a framework that resembles ribs in shape and function. The vaulting ribs of the "fan" vaults suggest the intricacy of fans; peculiar to English Perpendicular Gothic.

BIBLIOGRAPHY

DANIEL-ROPS, HENRI (ed.). *The Miracle of Ireland.* Translated by the Earl of Wicklow. Baltimore: Helicon Press, Inc., 1959.

DÉCARREAUX, J. *Les Moines et la Civilisation.* Paris: Arthaud, 1961.

GILSON, ETIENNE. *History of Christian Philosophy in the Middle Ages.* New York: Random House, Inc., 1955.

GRIVOT, DENIS and GEORGE ZARNECKI. *Gislebertus, Sculptor of Autun.* Paris: Trianon Press, 1961.

GROUSSET, RENÉ. *Bilan de l'Histoire.* Paris: Plon, 1948.

HALECKI, OSCAR, *The Limits and Divisions of European History.* New York: Sheed and Ward, Inc., 1950.

HÜRLIMANN, MARTIN and JEAN BONY. *French Cathedrals.* New York: Viking Press, Inc., 1951.

JANTZEN, HANS. *High Gothic.* New York: Pantheon Books, Inc., 1962.

MOULD, D. D. C. P. *Irish Pilgrimage.* New York: The Devin-Adair Company, 1957.

PEROWNE, STEWART. *Hadrian.* New York: W. W. Norton and Company, Inc., 1960.

PORTER, ARTHUR KINGSLEY. *The Crosses and Culture of Ireland.* New Haven: The Yale University Press, 1931.

DE REYNOLD, GONZAGUE. *La Formation de l'Europe.* Paris: Plon, 1957.

SAYERS, DOROTHY. *Four Sacred Plays.* London: Gollancz, 1948.

VON SIMSON, OTTO. *The Gothic Cathedral.* New York: Pantheon Books, Inc., 1956.

VAUGHAN, AGNES. C. *Bury Me in Ravenna.* Garden City: Doubleday and Company, Inc., 1962.

RECOMMENDED READING

*The following books are listed with their present, rather than original, publishers but with the original publication date. An asterisk * denotes a paperback edition.*

PRACTICAL GUIDE BOOKS

GENERAL

CLARK, SYDNEY. *All the Best in Europe.* New York: Dodd, Mead and Company, 1961. (Revised edition.)

FODOR, EUGENE (ed.) *Jet Age Guide to Europe.* New York: David McKay Company, Inc., 1961. (Revised edition.) A synthetic work, including the best of at least a dozen volumes edited by Fodor. Maps, city plans, and detailed information for each important city, together with essays written with broad sympathy, make this a very satisfactory, all-purpose guide.

FROMMER, ARTHUR. *Europe on $5 a Day.** New York: Crown Publishers, 1962. (Revised edition.) An inexpensive paperback that almost lives up to its title, offering every conceivable suggestion on how to live and travel economically, what snares to avoid, and the like.

JOSEPH, RICHARD. *Richard Joseph's Comprehensive Guide to Europe.* Garden City: Doubleday and Company, Inc., 1961. (Revised edition.)

NEWMAN, HAROLD. *Newman's European Travel Guide.* New York: Harper and Row, 1963. (Revised edition.)

OLSON, HARVEY S. *Aboard and Abroad.* Philadelphia: J. B. Lippincott Company, 1959, (Revised edition.)

PIERCE, ELEANOR. *New Horizons: Living Abroad.* New York: Pan American Airways, 1961.

STEIN, HOWARD and ADELAIDE. *The Budget Guide to Europe.* Princeton: D. Van Nostrand Company, Inc., 1962.

INDIVIDUAL COUNTRIES

"Baedeker Guide Book Series." New York: The Macmillan Company. This famous series is being thoroughly revised and given a new, flexible format. At present only a few countries are covered.

CLARK, SIDNEY. "All the Best in . . . Series." New York: Dodd, Mead and Company.

"The Blue Guides." Edited by L. Russell Muirhead and distributed by Rand McNally and Company, Chicago.

"Hachette World Guides." Edited and published by Librarie Hachette, Paris. Two English editions of the "Guide Bleu Series" which are detailed (maps included) and authoritative.

"Holiday Magazine Travel Guide Series." Edited by *Holiday* and published by Random House, Inc., New York.

"Michelin Green Guides." Edited and published by Michelin et Compagnie, Clermont-Ferrand. English editions of the "Guides Michelin." Particularly useful for the various parts of France. They include maps, charts, and much practical and historical information in a handy, flexible format.

Remember that almost all the information you will need—including excellent maps—will be provided free of charge by the national tourist offices of Western European countries. The publications of the government of France are works of art. (One of them is especially devoted to pilgrimages.)

"Visit Scandinavia" and "Holy Men and Women of Scandinavia," two brief useful bulletins, are available for a few cents from St. Ansgar's League, 40 W. 13th St., New York 11, N.Y.

BACKGROUND MATERIAL

HISTORICAL

D'ARCY, MARTIN C., S.J. *The Meaning and Matter of History.** Cleveland: The World Publishing Co., Inc. (Meridian), 1959. Fine material for meditation.

DAWSON, CHRISTOPHER. *The Making of Europe.** Cleveland: The World Publishing Co., Inc. (Meridian), 1945.

————. *Understanding Europe.** New York: Doubleday and Company, Inc. (Image Books), 1952.

————. *Religion and the Rise of Western Culture.** New York: Doubleday and Company, Inc. (Image Books), 1950. These and other works by Dawson are difficult to match as background material.

WARD, BARBARA. *Faith and Freedom.** New York: Doubleday and Company, Inc. (Image Books), 1954.

RELIGIOUS

DANIEL-ROPS, HENRI (ed.). *Twentieth Century Encyclopedia of Catholicism.* New York: Hawthorn Books, Inc., 1958—. Published in 150 volumes: offers excellent treatments of Church history and Christian culture.

DANIEL-ROPS, HENRI. *The Church in the Dark Ages.** Translated by Audrey Butler. New York: Doubleday and Company, Inc. (Image Books), 1959. Throws light on a difficult but important period of Church history.

HUGHES, PHILIP. *A History of the Church.* New York: Sheed and Ward, Inc., 1934.

————. *A Popular History of the Catholic Church.** New York: Doubleday and Company, Inc. (Image Books). Brief, classic introduction to Church history.

CULTURAL

CHRISTENSEN, ERWIN O. *The History of Western Art.** New York: The New American Library of World Literature, Inc. (Mentor), 1959. Bountifully illustrated and easy to carry: an extraordinary value.

GLOAG, JOHN. *Guide to Western Architecture.** New York: Grove Press, Inc. (Evergreen Books), 1958. A vividly written, balanced history and introduction to architecture, with four hundred illustrations.

SMITH, G. E. KIDDER. *The New Architecture of Europe.** Cleveland: The World Publishing Company, Inc. (Meridian), 1961. A guide to present-day building, well illustrated.

MÂLE, EMILE. *Religious Art: from the Twelfth to the Eighteenth Centuries.** New York: Farrar, Straus and Cudahy, Inc. (Noonday Paperbacks), 1949. Probably the leading general work on the subject.

MOREY, C. R. *Christian Art.* * New York: W. W. Norton & Co., Inc., 1935. A classic work on the subject.

NEWTON, ERIC. *European Painting and Sculpture.* * Baltimore: Penguin Books, Inc., 1942. An introduction by one of the sanest of art critics.

STADLER, WOLFGANG. *European Art: A Traveller's Guide.* New York: Herder and Herder, 1960. Includes 450 illustrations, many diagrams and maps: a book to study before and after your trip.

WATKINS, E. I. *Catholic Art and Culture.* New York: Sheed and Ward, Inc., 1941. A profound and readable work by one of the great minds of our time.

READING IN DEPTH

Certain literary works will help enrich your background and give you the "feel" of particular countries and cities, as well as of Europe generally.

ADAMS, HENRY. *Mont-Saint-Michel and Chartres.** New York: The New American Library of World Literature Inc. (Mentor), 1913. The perfect instance of interpretative reading.

BELLOC, HILAIRE. *The Path to Rome.** New York: Doubleday and Company, Inc. (Image Books), 1902. A classic of urbane, rambling prose, with the deepest feeling for Italy and Rome: rich in background and meaning.

BOWEN, ELIZABETH. *A Time in Rome.* New York: Alfred A. Knopf, Inc., 1959. Written with the delicacy and warmth of an important novelist who loves what she sees.

JAMES, HENRY. Selections in *The Art of Travel.** Edited with an introduction by Morton Dauwen Zabel. New York: Doubleday and Company, Inc. (Anchor), 1950. Collected writings on travel in Europe by an ardent voyager—a "passionate pilgrim," as James is sometimes called.

MENEN, AUBREY. *Rome for Ourselves.* New York: McGraw-Hill Book Company, 1960.

———. *Speaking the Language Like a Native.* New York: McGraw-Hill Book Company, 1962. Written with perception, irony and wit.

MORTON, H. V. *A Traveller in Rome.* New York: Dodd, Mead and Company, 1957.

———. *A Stranger in Spain.* New York: Dodd, Mead and Company, 1955.

———. *In Search of . . .* (four volumes—Scotland, Ireland, England, London). New York: Dodd, Mead and Company, 1927—. All models of perceptive, sympathetic observation that will help you prepare and later reminisce fruitfully.

O'FAOLAIN, SEAN. *A Summer in Italy*. New York: The Devin-Adair Company, 1950. Offers helpful insights.

SITWELL, SACHEVERELL. *Spain*.* New York: W. W. Norton and Company, Inc., 1950.

————. *Portugal and Madeira*. London: B. T. Batsford, 1954. Atmospheric writing in the best sense.

SWEENEY, FRANCIS (ed.). *Vatican Impressions*. New York: Sheed and Ward, 1962. An exceptionally useful anthology of European impressions, representing fortynine authors from Montaigne to Graham Greene.

NOVELS

Novels can illuminate a country or an epoch even more than formal studies.

GIRONELLA, JOSÉ MARÍA. *The Cypresses Believe in God*. Translated by Harriet de Onis. New York: Alfred A. Knopf, Inc., 1955. For a grasp of modern Spain in all its complex breadth and depth.

NOVAK, MICHAEL. *The Tiber Was Silver*. Garden City: Doubleday and Company, Inc., 1962. For an understanding of contemporary Rome.

PRESCOTT, H. F. M. *The Man on a Donkey*.* New York and London: The Macmillan Company, 1952. Superb preparatory reading.

WAUGH, EVELYN. *Helena*.* New York: Doubleday and Company, Inc. (Image Books), 1950. Ancient Christian Rome. Masterly.

PICTORIAL STUDIES

"Beaux Pays Series." Oxford: The Oxford University Press. A many-volumed series which includes a fine text.

FREMANTLE, ANNE. *Holiday in Europe*. Photographs by Fritz Hemle. New York: Viking Press, Inc., 1963. Combines intelligent, sensitive comment with fine photographs.

ROTKIN, CHARLES E. *Europe: An Aerial Close-Up*. Philadelphia: J. B. Lippincott Company, 1962. An unusual work. As the view is from the air, however, it may not prove as useful as Miss Fremantle's study.

INDEX

THE AUTHOR AND HIS BOOK

C. J. McNASPY, S.J., *historian, musicologist, connoisseur of art is Associate Editor of* America *and* Catholic Mind. *He received his A.B., M.A., Ph.L., and S.T.L. from St. Louis University, Missouri, his doctorate in Music from Montreal University and later did advanced work in Cultural History under Christopher Dawson at Oxford. He was formerly Dean of Music at Loyola University, New Orleans. As Professor of Art, Music, Languages, and History he has lectured in university classrooms and on television, and broadcasts weekly on New York FM radio his own program* Styles of Music. *A versatile writer, Father McNaspy has contributed several hundred articles, scholarly and familiar, to prominent journals here and abroad, written two best-selling pamphlets,* Let's Talk Sense about the Negro *and* The Vernacular Re-viewed.